Black Students–Middle-Class Teachers

By Jawanza Kunjufu

African American Images
Chicago, Illinois

Front cover illustration by Ed Bunch

First Edition, Sixth Printing

Printed in the United States of America

ISBN: 0-913543-81-0

What Does God Say About His Children?

At that time the disciples came to Jesus, saying, "Who then is the greatest in the Kingdom of Heaven?" Then Jesus called a little child to Him, set him in the midst of them, and said, "Assuredly I say unto you unless you are converted and become as little children, you by no means will enter the Kingdom of Heaven. Therefore whomever humbles himself as this little child is the greatest in the Kingdom of Heaven. Whomever receives one little child like this in My name receives Me. Whomever causes one of these little ones who believe in Me to sin, it would be better for him if a millstone were hung around his neck, and he would drown in the depth of the sea." Matthew 18:1-6

What you do unto the least of these you also do unto Me. Matthew 25:40

Scriptures from the *Life Application Bible,* New King James version.

Dedication

This book is dedicated to all African American students, whether they come from low- income or middle-income families, live in the inner city or suburbs, or attend schools with Black, White, or racially mixed staff. They are all struggling to receive a quality education. Due to the change in the economy from agriculture to manufacturing to the computer, this is the first generation of students where a quality education is a necessity. A portion of the proceeds of this book will support the education of African American students. Upon receipt of your school order, we will donate 30 percent of the sale to your students.

Contents

Trends

African American students comprise 17 percent of the U.S. student population.

African American teachers comprise 6 percent of U.S. teachers.

African American males comprise 1 percent of U.S. teachers.

White females comprise 83 percent of U.S. elementary teachers.

There is no staff of color in 44 percent of schools.

America's three million teachers will need to be replaced within two decades, primarily due to retirement.

Of African American teachers, 37 percent graduated from historically Black colleges and universities.

Of inner city teachers, 40 percent transfer within five years.

Over 40 percent of public school teachers send their children to private schools.

In most states, the most affluent school district allocates $18,000 per child while only $5,000 is allocated in the least affluent school district.

The national average per pupil school expenditure is $7,682.

In the state of New York, one district allocates $38,572 per pupil while the least affluent school district only allocates $6,100.

Students lose 80 percent of what they learned during the school year when off 12 weeks during the summer. A better alternative is 9 weeks in and 3 weeks off.

Full day kindergarten has greatly improved academic performance.

In Ohio, the wealthiest school district allocates $24,160 per pupil while the lowest funded school district only allocates $3,345.

African American children comprise 17 percent of the student population but constitute almost 40 percent of students placed in various categories of special education.

If an African American child is placed in special education, 80 percent of the time the child will be male.

One of every three African American males is involved with a penal institution while only one of ten male high-school graduates is enrolled in college.

Only 3 percent of African American students is placed in gifted and talented programs.

Almost 80 percent of referrals to special education is generated by 20 percent of teachers.

Of American students, 6 percent are referred to special education, 92 percent of that number is tested, and 73 percent of that number is placed.

There are four million children receiving Ritalin, one million before third grade. Twelve percent of American public school students are placed in special education.

Sixty-three percent of African American fourth grade students is below grade level in reading. Over 80 percent of inmates entered prison illiterate. States project prison growth based on fourth grade reading levels.

Sixty-one percent of eighth grade African American students is below grade level in math.

Thirty-three percent of African American households lives below the poverty line.

Twenty-five percent of African American households earns more than $50,000 per year.

Eighty percent of all children feels good about school in kindergarten, 20 percent in fifth grade, and only 5 percent in high school.

In light of Brown vs. Topeka in 1954, schools have become more segregated since 1971.

Ninety-eight percent of African American children attends public schools.

There are an estimated two million children home schooled, with 50,000 in African American homes.

On the SAT, 5,303 African American females and 2,603 African American males scored better than 1200.

Fifty-three million children attend American schools. Forty-eight million students attend public schools. Nine percent of American students attend private schools. Only 1 percent of American students attend charter schools or use vouchers.

The media reports that 83 percent of African Americans graduate from high school. The reality is only 56 percent. Most major cities have a dropout rate of 40 percent. Accounting for the statistical difference of 27 percent is the fact that African Americans earn their GED before age 25 in spite of the school system.

By 2035, children of color will be the majority population.[1]

Introduction

I have been an educational consultant to school districts for almost 30 years. I have provided in-service training for teachers in the inner-city, suburbs, and rural communities. Unfortunately, the racial achievement gap persists regardless of the geographical region. It remains visible in spite of the income or marital status of the parents. In addition, the achievement disparity transcends the racial makeup of the teachers.

On the Scholastic Achievement Test (SAT), there is a 200 point differential. On K-8 achievement tests there is almost a three stanine difference between White and Black children. The major objective of this book is to provide strategies to improve the academic achievement of African American students. This book is primarily written for teachers, but I included a chapter for parents. I respect and appreciate principals who invite parents to their staff meetings. If we seriously want to close the achievement gap, we must empower parents and increase communication between staff and parents.

One of the major catalysts for writing this book came from a principal's comment. She told me that in her school the problem was not a shortage of African American teachers but their class and value conflict with the students. She described her frustration of observing middle-class African American teachers being condescending toward low-income students. Another objective of the book is to describe this value conflict.

My third objective is to empower White teachers. The future of African American students lies in the hands of White teachers. The trends illustrate the dearth of African American teachers. Since Brown vs. Topeka (1954) and the integration of schools, there has been a 66 percent decline in African Americans pursuing teaching. Eighty-three percent of all elementary school teachers are White females.

At the end of this introduction are two quizzes on multiculturalism and inclusion. I think it is unfortunate that many White teachers of African American students have never lived in the Black community and never took a college course on Black history, culture, learning styles, or Ebonics. Ironically, many African American teachers also fail the quizzes because while they live in the Black community and attended African American colleges, the curriculum remained Eurocentric.

The next objective of the book is specifically to improve the achievement of middle-income African American students. Ironically, the gap is wider between middle-income White and Black students. Regardless of African American family income, education challenges remain constant: lower teacher expectations, a boring irrelevant Eurocentric curriculum, a disproportionate percentage of left-brain lesson plans, tracking, and negative peer pressure that discourages African American achievement.

Throughout the book I provide solutions, but the last chapter, Models of Success, provides a convenient, comprehensive analysis that addresses the objectives. I have no loyalty to unions, White or Black educators, school boards, or other vested interests. I am only concerned with the academic achievement of African American students. Solutions may come from organizations as disparate as the Brookings Institute and the Council of Independent Institutions.

I thank you for reading the book and I pray you do well on the quizzes!

Multicultural Quiz

1. How do African American children define good hair and pretty eyes?
2. Why do many African American youth associate beauty with light skin?
3. What are the benefits of dark skin?
4. Name some classical musicians and writers.
5. Why do some African American youth associate being smart with acting White?
6. Why don't Whites associate being smart with acting Black?
7. At what age do Jewish parents and educators teach their children about the Holocaust?
8. At what age do parents and educators of African American children teach them about slavery?
9. From a multicultural perspective, what is the difference between a salad bowl and a melting pot?
10. Why did twentieth-century European immigrants melt into American society faster than African Americans?
11. What makes countries Third World? What are the first and second worlds?
12. Who built the Pyramids? When were they built? When was the zenith of Greek civilization?
13. What is standard English?
14. Did Oakland schools want to teach African American students Ebonics?
15. What is code switching?
16. What percentage of the world population is White?
17. What is the one-drop-of-blood theory?
18. How many Whites live below the poverty line in America?
19. What percentage of drug users and drug convictions involve Whites?
20. Which day of the week and hour are the most segregated in America?
21. Do you have different opinions when you see four African American male teens in the school hallway versus four White male teens?
22. What is the difference between a group and a gang? Between being assertive and aggressive?

Inclusion Quiz

Fill in the blanks with the names of the most appropriate African Americans who worked or lived during the same era.

White	African American
Abraham Lincoln	_____
Thomas Edison	_____
Alexander Bell	_____
Hippocrates	_____
Eleanor Roosevelt	_____
J.F. Kennedy	_____

Chapter One

Middle-Class Schools

❖ Can middle-income teachers educate low-income children?

❖ Two consecutive years of bad teaching could destroy a child for life.

❖ A child has a much greater chance of being placed in special education or tracked in remedial classes if he or she doesn't look or speak like the teacher.

❖ Is the ideal student one who can sit still for long periods of time, quietly working by himself on irrelevant ditto sheets?

❖ School is the first place where most children learn how to fail.

❖ One of the best ways to evaluate a school is by the conversation in the teachers' lounge.

❖ If we believe all children can learn, then why do so many adults accept studies describing the plight of low-income, fatherless, African American children?

❖ Do schools educate, level, track, or mis-educate?

❖ Is "different" synonymous with "deficient"?

❖ Are schools designed for *Leave It to Beaver* children or *Bebe's Kids*?

❖ Schools reward incompetence. The longer teachers perform poorly, the more they are compensated.

❖ How can public school teachers who send their children to private schools be against choice?

❖ Would you, as a teacher, teach differently if your child were in your classroom? Why?

❖ Does your child attend the school where you teach? If not, why? Are you in favor of choice?

❖ Do we have at-risk schools or at-risk students?

❖ Do we have bad children or poor classroom management?

❖ Are there different schools for employees and employers?

❖ The inadequate training of teachers is the single most debilitating force at work in American schools.

❖ Most schools do a poor job of handling Black male energy.

❖ Are educators only trained to teach motivated students?

❖ Remember that 95 percent of discipline problems occur during the first and last five minutes of the class and come from 5 percent of the students.

❖ When schools retain students but do not change teachers' expectations, time on task, pedagogy, or curriculum but expect better results, it borders on insanity.

❖ In low-income schools, good behavior is valued more than learning.

❖ Attention deficit disorder (ADD) has been around ever since teachers have attempted to instruct students on issues in which they have no interest. It should be defined as a teaching disability rather than a learning disability.

❖ Ineffective teachers use an outdated curriculum and pedagogy to produce inmates.

❖ The racial academic achievement gap is non-existent when we compare White students from their best school to African Americans from their best school. We have a *school* problem not a Black student problem.

Thirty-three percent of African American households live below the poverty line, which is defined as a family of four earning less than $15,000 per year. Twenty-five percent of African

Middle-Class Schools

American households earn more than $50,000 a year. The majority of African American households, 42 percent, earn between $15,000 and $50,000 a year.

The above figures don't tell the entire story, however. The reality is that 50 percent of African American children live below the poverty line. That is because most African American low-income households have more than the middle-class average of 1.8 children. I wrote this book because of the increasing number of African American children living below the poverty line and the conflict they experience in values—middle-class schools vs. low-income African American children.

The working class population represents 42 percent of the African American community. The combination of 50 percent below the poverty line and 42 percent in the working class adds up to 92 percent of African American children living either below the poverty line or in the working class community. Therefore, only 8 percent of African American children come from middle-class households earning above $50,000. Some of the differences in how these children and households function are as follows:

Category	Under class	Working class	Middle class
Housing	Public housing	Apartment	House
Transportation	Bus	Sub-compact car	Luxury car
Geography	Inner city	Outskirts of city	Suburbs
School	Neighborhood school	Magnet school	Private school
Personal Finance	Money orders	Checking account	Stock market
Entertainment	Television	Video games	Computer/Internet

The title of this book, *Black Students–Middle-Class Teachers,* doesn't make a distinction between low-income

Black students and middle-income Black students. Many African American children, whether they attend inner city schools or suburban schools, suffer academically. In 66 percent of African American households, the father is not present. The implications from an educational standpoint are numerous. Most PTA meetings or parent-staff conferences will only have the mother in attendance. If she works a shift that conflicts with the school's schedule, the child may go without adult representation. One parent's attention must be spread among several siblings. There is only so much homework assistance that one parent can provide to several children. In addition, mother must cook and maintain the household after a full day of working.

I've also found that all African American children, regardless of income, are susceptible to the peer group, which all too often discourages academic achievement. In one of my earlier books, *To Be Popular or Smart: The Black Peer Group*, I discussed the tremendous negative impact of peer pressure on academic achievement. Most families assume that because they are not lower class or fatherless children will perform well in school. This misconception has been especially frustrating for middle-income families, schools, and school districts that have high levels of low-performing students. Negative peer pressure discourages almost all African American youth from participating in advance placement, honors, and gifted and talented classes unless getting on the honor roll is easy and doesn't require additional study time. Natural ability may sustain students in the primary grades, but from fourth grade on, only hard work and discipline will lead to high honors.

One of the major conflicts between middle-class values and low-income values is the dichotomy between "we" and "me."

Middle-Class Schools

Middle-class values encourage individuals to separate themselves from the group to pursue their personal aspirations. But whether the African American child attends a suburban school or an inner city school, he or she wants to be part of the peer group. If the peer group discourages participation in the science fair, debate team, or German club, then most African American students will get involved in other social pursuits. Visit an inner city elementary or high school and then visit a predominantly African American suburban elementary or high school and you will see little difference in the quality of peer pressure. Many parents in middle-class communities think that by moving to the suburbs they'd see improvement in their children's academic achievement. They thought they'd escape the negative peer pressure. Unfortunately, it exists everywhere.

Let's now look at the school as an institution and describe some middle-class behaviors of the school, which conflict with the values and behaviors of many African American students. Homework is one way that schools demonstrate middle-class values. I was taught as a former teacher never to assign homework that I would not thoroughly review in class. If a teacher reviews problems 1 through 10 but assigns problems 11 through 20 for homework and the latter problems have an additional step that was not discussed in problems 1-10 the teacher literally is expecting the parent to become the assistant teacher and to educate her child about that additional step. This is unfair, and with each succeeding grade homework increases and becomes more challenging.

In addition, middle-class teachers expect that all homes will have what they have in their homes. Not every African American household possesses an encyclopedia set, atlas, globe, extensive library, computer, color printer, and Internet access. It is unfair for teachers to give assignments for which these materials are expected and required. It is also unfair to favor children with access to these materials and reward them with credit and better grades. I've heard school horror stories of children receiving extra credit because their reports were typed and included color graphics. This scenario does not evaluate the child's learning but rather the household's assets.

Often, schools will give children an assignment that necessitates a visit to the public library, museum, planetarium, aquarium, or some other cultural institution. It is unfortunate that many African American parents associate field trips with schools. I would encourage my readers to visit these institutions and see if the percentage of African Americans there is comparable to that of the city itself. Is it fair to lower the student's grade because the parent does not take his or her child to one of those institutions? Is it fair to expect a working-class or low-income single parent without a car to take his or her child to one of these institutions? Are teachers aware that many gang-infested neighborhoods are on "lockdown"? When gangs go to war, all families are expected to stay inside their homes.

Many parents tell me that teachers advise them to seek counseling, tutoring, and medical assistance for their children. Although this is not a financial problem for middle-income families, it is a challenge for impoverished and working-class families. Middle-class educators are also wrong to assume that the government provides all these services freely.

Conflict resolution styles differ between the cultures. Middle-class teachers expect students to tell them when someone has committed a violation. Black parents, regardless of class, believe in "an eye for an eye." On the street, the code is retaliation, not "snitching." In addition, African American students will divulge their secrets only when teachers have earned their trust.

In her book, *Framework for Understanding Poverty*, Ruby Payne talks about the communication styles of classes. Payne describes the conflict as the "formal register" versus the "casual register." Middle-class schools expect everyone to speak in the formal register. Achievement tests are written in the formal register. From a middle-class perspective the ability or inability to speak in the formal register, which entails complete sentences and an expanding vocabulary, is one of the major ways students are evaluated. In contrast, the casual register has a more limited vocabulary, sentence structure is incomplete, and slang is a major part of the vernacular.[2] The Black peer group believes you are "acting White" when you speak in the formal register. Much more will be said about this in subsequent chapters.

One divisive tool of middle-class schools is the Individual Educational Plan (IEP). In my opinion, the IEP is one of the most important meetings of a child's school career. It is designed to determine whether the child will be placed in special education. Previously, we mentioned that 6 percent of all children are referred to special education, and of these 92 percent will be tested and 73 percent will be placed. It is a vicious cycle once it begins.

The IEP meeting is intimidating, and most parents walk in totally unprepared and not knowing their rights. Visualize this scenario with me: The meeting is scheduled for 12:00 noon. Four professionals including the principal, psychologist, social worker, and teacher arrive at 11:30. They begin discussing whether the child should be placed in special education. From a middle-class perspective, punctuality is vital. If the meeting is scheduled for 12:00, that is the time it should start. Unfortunately, in low-income homes punctuality is not valued and the low-income single parent might arrive at 12:15. She feels like she has already been talked about, and she senses that the decision has already been made. The die has been cast. People who are entrenched in middle-class values become so self-centered that they cannot imagine what it is like to walk in her shoes. If only they knew scripture: "What you do unto the least of these you also do unto Me." Matthew 25:40.

Mother further compounds the problem when she speaks in the casual register, and heaven forbid if she dressed casually. Although the purpose of the meeting was to discuss the child, the mother is now the focus. The child loses points because the mother was late, did not speak in the formal register, and did not dress in middle-class attire.

One of the reasons this book is titled *"Black Students–Middle-Class Teachers* is because it is very possible that some of those professionals were African American. If the book had been titled "Black Students–White Teachers" or "Black Students–Middle-Class White Teachers," it would assume that if African American children were taught by African American educators the class phenomenon would not exist and African American students would be performing at a much higher level. This is not true and in subsequent chapters we will elaborate on the dynamics between race and class.

Ironically, at the IEP one or more of the four professionals could have been African American. Naively, the low-income, single, female parent thought that because one or more of the attendees were African American, they had an advocate who would help them and prevent their child from being placed in special education.

Middle-Class Schools

Unfortunately, in many of these scenarios, very similar to the police department, the code blue compromising attitude with the school is valued more than saving African American children. I commend all professionals who buck the system and advocate for African American children.

I once spoke at a conference of social workers and shared the IEP scenario. After my speech, an African American social worker approached me and said she resented my story. I understood her concerns and simply said that if the shoe does not fit there is no need to wear it. If you are an African American educator, social worker, psychologist, or principal and are not guilty of having sided with the school against the child when you knew in your heart that there were other possibilities that could and should have been considered, then there is no need for you to feel ashamed or guilty. Unfortunately, people who are self-centered can only evaluate events from their own perspective. I am aware of thousands of situations where African American professionals have sided with the organization over low-income African Americans.

Another illustration showing schools to be middle-class institutions is tracking. Schools divide children into ability groups, which is called tracking. The rationale has been that it's easier for teachers to work with homogeneous groups, and students benefit from associating with their "own kind." Conversely, it's frustrating for low-achieving students to be with higher achievers. Initially, this seems to make sense. However, excellent books have been written on this subject that show the destructive impact of tracking. I encourage you to read the works of Jeannie Oakes, Ray Rist, John Goodlad, and Jonathan Kozol.

Tracking widens the gap between the haves and have nots. Tracking begins very early in schools. In kindergarten, while they don't use terms like advanced placement, honors, and gifted and talented, they begin to divide children into such groups as eagles, robins, bluebirds, and chickens. It doesn't take long for children to realize that the eagles are better students. The achievement gap between the eagles and robins is much smaller in kindergarten than the achievement gap between eighth-grade honor students and remedial students. The children have been in school nine years between kindergarten and eighth grade, and over those nine years, due to tracking, the achievement gap has widened.

Politicians often say, "For the people, for the people." Likewise, educators say, "For the children, for the children." If education truly were for children, we would have abolished tracking long ago. Tracking is one of the worst practices that ever happen to students. Tracking is beneficial to teachers. I am very much aware that if we abolish tracking an eighth-grade teacher could possibly have ten students at a tenth-grade level, ten students at the eighth-grade level, and ten students at a fourth-grade level in their class. This would be very challenging for the teacher. But I am reminded of the construction sign that says, "We apologize for this short-term inconvenience for this long-term benefit." The reason why we have this wide disparity between fourth-grade and tenth-grade learning levels is because of the nine previous years during which tracking destroyed the students.

Tracking mirrors our economy and society. In schools you have the upper class, the middle class, and the lower class. The economy does not need schools to produce students who all have college degrees. If every student had a degree, who would work at McDonald's? If every student had a college degree, who would work as the custodians, secretaries, clerks, and other laborers? I used to believe that tracking was ineffective, but the more I read books on school history, such as Carter G. Woodson's *The Mis-Education of the Negro*, the more I realized that tracking is effective because schools never said they were going to educate all children. The mission of American schools is to mirror capitalism and produce winners and losers. And if that is the barometer, then tracking is effective because schools do produce winners and losers.

What's unfortunate is that as long as the Black middle class (including Black middle-class teachers) put their children in advanced placement, honors, gifted and talented classes, and magnet schools, they'll never see anything wrong with this elitist class system. This is analogous to life on the plantation and the relationship between "house" Negroes and "field" Negroes. If we accept the notion that it is beneficial for educators to teach homogenous groups and that it is also beneficial for students to be in homogenous groups, that doesn't dictate that higher-achieving students should receive the most experienced teachers and greater resources. If schools were truly interested in closing the achievement gap, then low-achieving students would receive the most experienced teachers and the greatest resources. But schools, which are controlled by the upper- and middle-class populations whose children are in the higher-achieving groups, have no intention of implementing such a policy. Ephesians 6:12 reads, "We struggle not against flesh and blood but against principalities, powers and rulers in high places." The demon that is driving tracking transcends race. If tracking were just a race issue, the Black middle class would be involved in abolishing tracking; but if the Black middle class benefits, then they side with the other beneficiaries to the detriment of low-income, low-achieving White, Asian, Black, Native American, and Hispanic students. This is more of a class than a race issue.

In a later chapter on Master Teachers, I'll describe how higher-achieving groups receive more experienced teachers and greater resources and how the pedagogy is different in the two classrooms. In high-achieving classes, students are being prepared to become employers and critical thinking skills are valued. In the low-achieving classes, students are being prepared to become employees.

Another illustration of the class dynamics that is taking place in education is the issue of school choice and vouchers. Is it fair that some parents are restricted to their one, local, under-performing school? Choice allows parents to choose a public school from throughout the city. Vouchers allow them to expand the universe and include private schools within the voucher dollar range. Why would a public school teacher be against low-income children receiving vouchers to attend the private school that their child presently attends? Who knows their school better than the teachers? Why would an educator not send their child to their school? Many teachers send their children to schools that have lower per student expenditures than the one in which they teach. Many private school pupil expenditures are actually smaller than public school. Their school pays higher salaries but, many teachers feel, offers an inferior education.

Low-income parents look to middle-class educators for solutions to solve educational problems in the African American community. It is very confusing to low-income parents to be told by African American educators that they need to stay with public schools while they send their own children to private schools. The two popular arguments against vouchers are that it is

Middle-Class Schools

Republican financed and that it will destroy public schools. I would encourage anyone who is serious about securing the truth on this issue to have a long conversation with Howard Fuller, the former school superintendent in Milwaukee, and his organization BAFEO (Black Alliance for Educational Options). Howard Fuller is in favor of choice and is not swayed by teacher unions. Why would a former superintendent of a public school system be in favor of choice? Fuller believes decisions should be made in the interest of children first – not unions, school boards, and politicians.

I said earlier that educators remind me of politicians, since, unfortunately, both groups serve their own interests. It does not surprise me that a public school educator would be against choice. What concerns me is the inconsistency of being against choice for low-income students while sending their own children to private schools. Are they against choice because they're afraid of losing their jobs? Do they want their own children to receive a better education? What kind of message does this send to low-income families? Those who are afraid that the Republican Party and the affluent will use vouchers to avoid sending their children to integrated public schools should be aware that most legislation only provides vouchers to low-income families.

Many educational and social activists fear that vouchers would destroy public schools. Private schools would pick and choose students, and the majority of low-income, low-achieving African American and Hispanic children would attend public schools that now have less money because it was siphoned off to private schools. I never quite understood that argument. If a school had 1,000 students and the per pupil expenditure was $6,000 and, with vouchers, 100 of their students were able to go to a private school, the school simply would have 900 students and the expenditure would still be $6,000 per child. Furthermore, since the voucher would not be $6,000 (they average about $3,000), the state would have extra money to allocate to fewer remaining students. If a greater percentage of the 900 needed special education, separate funds allocated for that program could be used. The answer to the argument that vouchers would siphon off better students is that this currently happens anyway by sending better students to magnet schools.

As an educational consultant to both public and private schools, I try to remain objective. For example: If I were a pastor and had a private school, people would assume that the reason why I am in favor of vouchers is because of my vested interest. If I were a public school educator and was against vouchers, people would assume that I wanted to keep my job. That's why I respect Howard Fuller. He has served as a public school superintendent and also worked in the private sector, so he brings a wealth of objectivity to the discussion.

When I think about vouchers, I think of the Council of Independent Black Institutions (CIBI) that was founded in 1972. This is a network of independent Africentric schools. Member schools would benefit greatly from vouchers. More will be said about CIBI in the last chapter on Models of Success. CIBI disputes the criticism that we have no viable educational institutions in the African American community. The takeover of Philadelphia schools by White corporations is not only a slap in the face to public schools but also African American churches, independent schools, and the entire Black community.

When I am forced to take a position on this subject, my response is that African American children need to attend the school that offers the best education. I am in favor of children attending public schools and prefer that teachers live in the city.

Middle-Class Schools

Their children should attend a public school, preferably where their parents teach. I believe educators teach more effectively when there is something at stake. Unfortunately, we have public school educators, White and Black, who do not live in the city in which they teach. Their children do not attend public school, and some believe they can mis-educate children without consequences because there is nothing at stake.

Middle-class schools have failed to prepare poor children for college admission. In some families children take the PSAT in eighth grade, visit many colleges, and make their college decision in their sophomore or junior year of high school. In other families the child takes the ACT or SAT in the spring of his or her senior year and applies for admission as late as July or August. In some schools there is a 50-1 ratio between students and counselors. Other schools have a ratio of 500-1. There are some schools where every scholarship known to man has been identified and secured. There are other schools where the word scholarship is so rare that it is seldom mentioned and never secured. Middle-class el-hi schools provide a college prep curriculum for their students. Test-taking skills are taught and scholarship money is abundant. Low-income schools prepare their students for fast-food chains and Wal-Mart. The college admission process is a maze. It requires a great degree of persistence and attention to detail to complete applications, secure transcripts, and provide test scores within the proper guidelines and deadlines.

Lastly, I think time is the great divide between middle-class schools and African American students. Education is based on the value of long-term gratification. If you can endure 13 years between kindergarten and twelfth grade, there will be a rainbow upon graduation, which is a college scholarship. If you endure four years of college, you will receive a good job. If you persevere through graduate school, you will be rewarded with an even more lucrative position. One of the major values of the middle-class is their ability to delay gratification. Unfortunately, many African American students have short attention spans. They also lack confidence in the promise of a college scholarship, a good job, and a lucrative career. Principals of schools in high unemployment areas must create partnerships with the limited business community to convince youth to graduate. This partnership must promise and provide employment.

In a later chapter on African American students, I'll discuss in more detail how many African American youth believe their chances in life are better in the NBA, signing a rap contract, or becoming a drug dealer. This is further reinforced when African American youth observe African American college graduates who are unemployed, underemployed, or underpaid. It becomes even a greater conflict when African American youth observe drug dealers who earn much more money than African Americans with college degrees. We must convince African American youth that they have a much better chance in a classroom than on the streets. The question is, how will we convince them?

Peter Murrell, Jr., in *African Centered Pedagogy* argues that the national concern about the "achievement gap" places the onus on African American children and the high stakes of culturally biased standardized achievement tests. The fundamental problem is that schools have not provided quality Africentric teaching to African American children.

In the next chapter we will look at White female teachers. The future of the Black race lies in their hands. They constitute 83 percent of the elementary teaching force.

Chapter Two

White Female Teachers

❖ "I don't see color. I treat all children the same. I see children as children."

❖ "'These kids' are not like the ones we used to have."

The future of the African American population primarily lies in the hands of White female teachers. Ninety-three percent of the American teaching staff is White. Eighty-three percent of elementary school teachers are White females; the percentage of White males increases in junior and senior high schools.

As an educational consultant to hundreds of schools nationwide over the past three decades, I have witnessed the declining percentage of African American teachers and the increasing percentage of African American students. I now find myself spending the largest percentage of my time providing in-service training for White female teachers on how to better serve African American students. When I first became a consultant in 1974, I did a lot of work in the inner city with African American teachers. Today, as African Americans migrate all over the country, I find myself working in the inner city, suburbia, and rural areas. Many suburbs have a large African American student population, but few African American teachers. These schools are crying for more African American teachers.

I believe that the most important factor impacting the academic achievement of African American children is not the race or gender of the teacher but the teacher's expectations. If I did not believe this, the title of this book would have been "Black Students–White Teachers" and I would have narrowed my focus to these two groups.

I have provided in-service training in many school districts where both students and staff were African American, and test scores were abysmal. On the other hand, I've been in school districts where the children were African American and the staff was White, and test scores were above the national average. It's too simplistic to say that the teacher's race is the determining factor impacting academic achievement. In the next chapter on African American teachers, we will look at the controversial research of Thomas Dee, who suggests that a teacher's race is the most important factor. I believe the teacher's expectations is the most important reason why children excel or fail in school.

I would encourage everyone reading this book to read the work of Lois Weiner and Karen Teel. They address the fact that many White teachers grew up in rural areas or lived their entire lives in White neighborhoods. They attended a White university, worshipped in a White church, and shopped in White grocery stores. They did their student teaching in rural school districts and accepted teaching assignments in the inner city. Many White male and female teachers who are now attempting to educate African American children have not taken one course in African American history, culture, family, learning styles, or Ebonics. Consequently, they are ill prepared to work with African American children, and I don't believe it is their fault. How could a teacher who grew up in a White rural community and was educated in a White environment be effective in the inner cities of America?

How can we expect a teacher from that environment to "code switch" between standard English and Ebonics without placing a negative value on the latter? I define code switching as allowing a child to speak or write first in the "dialect of comfort." The teacher will then ask the child to restate or rewrite in standard English. This request is made positively without putting a negative connotation on the former. They view the children as bilingual.

White Female Teachers

Were Oakland schools trying to teach Black children Ebonics? Just think about that for a moment. Don't Black children already know Ebonics? Oakland's objective was to provide cultural diversity training to their increasingly White staff, which should have been provided by university education departments. Oakland schools had no intention of teaching African American children Ebonics. They had every intention of teaching incoming staff how to code switch. I would like you to review your answers on the multicultural quiz. How well did you do? How well did your education department prepare you for these questions? What was the extent of the in-service training that you received from your school as it relates to these questions? How frequently do you interact with African American staff if they are available to discuss these issues? Can a person be a multicultural teacher if they are not a multicultural person? Can a person be multicultural from 9:00 until 3:00 Monday through Friday and racist on the weekend?

I have observed schools that celebrate "multicultural day," when students are asked to come to school in their native attire, bring ethnic food and music, and say a few words in their native language. I strongly suggest that to be a multicultural teacher requires much more than that. It requires applying your understanding of another culture to your curriculum and pedagogy. It necessitates respect, tolerance, and a willingness to learn from your students.

In my workshops, one of the concepts we discuss is the "showdown." It is a power struggle, a rites of passage between African American male students and female teachers. I wonder if there is one education department in America that prepares teachers for the showdown? I believe it is impossible to teach a child if you are afraid of him or her. Ironically, African American males want the teacher to win the showdown, but if they ever notice fear, you have lost their respect and can no longer be an effective teacher. How unfortunate that I give workshops for teachers with years of experience and it is the first time they gain an understanding of the showdown. Teachers in the primary division can use their size to discipline students, but from the fourth grade on, size is irrelevant. Many boys in the intermediate, upper, and high school grades are taller than their teachers.

Earlier we mentioned that 40 percent of inner city staff quit within five years. We could reduce this rate if we better prepared teachers in college education departments. I often wonder if education professors have ever taught in the inner city. Many education departments have prepared teachers for *Leave It to Beaver* children and not *Bebe's Kids*. I encourage every education professor to read the works of Peter Murrell, Jr., James Banks, Michele Foster, Gloria Ladson-Billings, Carol Lee, Mwalimu Shujaa, Jacqueline Irvine, Janice Hale, Asa Hillard, Lisa Delpit, Linda Darling-Hammond, and the retired Barbara Sizemore. These are some of the best Africentric educators.

One of my most challenging workshops was presented to a school district that was in racial transition. The predominately White teaching staff had been there for more than twenty years and spoke about the good old days when almost all the children were White. When White residents in the neighborhood took flight, White students also departed, but White teachers remained. African Americans had taken over the school and community. The principal invited me to speak to the teachers to give them strategies on how to maximize the achievement of African American students. The problem was that the teachers viewed the students as "these children" and felt that I needed to fix the children and their parents. They felt nothing needed modification

White Female Teachers

on their part, and the proof was that in the good old days of White teachers and White students everything was fine—the children were disciplined and academically above the national average.

I encourage all White teachers to read the work of Gary Howard and Vivian Paley. These White authors attempt to soothe the nerves of White teachers in these kinds of settings. I've been in some workshops where you could cut the tension with a knife. In the book *We Can't Teach What We Don't Know: White Teacher Multi-Racial Schools* author Gary Howard describes an in-service he was conducting. The teachers were annoyed at having to attend another workshop on multiculturalism and race relations. He mentions that to be successful with this type of group, you must be delicate and not blame them.[3] Rodney King asks, "Can't we all just get along?" No. We can't get along until we know the truth and, as the Bible teaches us in John 8:32, " The truth will make you free." The question becomes, do White teachers want to know the truth?

While many Whites want the children to be "fixed," others simply leave, transferring to White districts. I have heard, "I have two years, four months, two weeks, three days, four hours, and seventeen minutes before retirement." Others deceive themselves and say they are "liberal." They say, "I don't see color, I see children as children, and I treat them all the same." I often ask those liberal teachers after my workshop if I can visit their classroom. I believe bulletin boards, lesson plans, and library collections don't lie. I expect to see a multicultural bulletin board, library collection, and lesson plans that reflect the cultural mosaic of their students. Unfortunately, what I have observed is a predominantly all White "Dick and Jane" bulletin board, library collection, and lesson plans; yet they say they do not see color. I believe they see it better than anyone else does.

The first step is to admit that race is a factor. The second step is to understand race or ethnicity by reading the history and culture of your students. It disappoints me when I work with a school district with an increasing number of African American children that there is resistance to learning about the group the teachers are being paid to educate.

The last step is to appreciate the culture. It is possible for someone to *look* Black but not *think* or *act* Black. Clarence Thomas and Ward Connerly are perfect illustrations of people who look African American but do not make decisions in the best interest of the African American community. Similarly, there are African American teachers who do not appreciate Black culture.

In the following chart, there are three categories of White identity orientations: Fundamentalist, Integrationist, and Transformationist. I would like you to review this chart and honestly ask yourself, "Which one am I?" Review the self-awareness section. Do you believe your perspective is the only correct one? Do you believe your perspective is one of many? Is your perspective changing?

White Female Teachers

WHITE IDENTITY ORIENTATIONS

	MODALITIES OF GROWTH	FUNDAMENTALIST	INTEGRATIONIST	TRANSFORMATIONIST
THINKING	Construction of Truth	Literal and fixed / Single-dimentional truth / Western-centric	Acknowledge diverse perspectives / Interest in broader truths / Continued defense of Western superiority	Legitimacy of diverse perspectives / Truth as dynamic/changing / Actively seeking divergent truths
	Construction of Whiteness	Supremacist/White is right / Ignorance/avoidance / Confusion	Beginning awareness / Some self-interrogation / Dissonance	Self-reflective critique / Deep interrogation of Whiteness / Affirming authentic/positive/nonracist identity
	Construction of Dominance	Legitimize/perpetuate dominance / Rationalize / Deny/ignore	Victim's perspective / Personal rather than institutional / critique of dominance	Acknowledge complicity / Holistic critique of oppression / Comprehensive analysis of dominance
	Level of Self-Awareness	My perspective is right – the only one / Self-esteem linked to supremacy / Threatened by differences	My perspective is one of many / Self-esteem linked to "helping" others / "Wannabe" phenomenon	My perspective is changing / Self-esteem linked to growth and change / I am enhanced by connection to different groups
INTERACTING	Emotional Response to Differences	Fear/hostility/avoidance / Judgment / Colorblindness	Interest / Beginning awareness / Cultural voyeurism/curiosity	Appreciation/respect / Enthusiasm/joy / Honesty
	Emotional Response to Discussions of Racism	Anger / Denial / Defensiveness/avoidance	Shame/guilt/confusion / Missionary zeal / Externalized as someone else's problem	Acknowledgment/empathy / Enlightened aversion to oppression / Responsibility without guilt
	Approach to Cross-Cultural Interactions	Distance/ilosation / Hostility / Reinforcing White superiority	Norrawly circumscribed/tentative / Patronizing / Emphasizing commanalities	Active seeking / Deeply personal/rewarding / Transforming/healing
HEALING	Approach to Teaching About Differences	Monocultural / Treat all students "the same" / Actively Eurocentric	Special program for special folks / Learning about other cultures / Tacitly Eurocentric	Social action/authentic engagement / Learning from other cultures / Challenging the Eurocentric perspective
	Approach to Leadership/Management	Autocratic/directive / Assimilationist / Perpetuates White dominance	Compliance oriented / Invite others into "our" house / Tacit support of White dominance	Advocacy / Collaboration/co-responsibility / Challenging/dismantling White dominance

During my workshops, we discuss curriculum, and I red flag key historical figures such as Columbus, Abraham Lincoln, and Hippocrates. This can become very unsettling for a Fundamentalist, who has no desire to change. They would rather keep their positions and resent learning new things about the children they teach. The popular joke is "don't confuse me with the facts." For the Fundamentalist in denial who believes his/her perspective is right and is the only perspective, it can become very challenging to them to hear that Columbus didn't discover America. Self-centered White people believe that until Europeans arrived here there was no America. It is even more unsettling to discover that Africans mastered the laws of math and science at such an advanced level that they were able to build pyramids without the assistance of Greek scholars. It is one thing not to know, and it is another when you do not want to know.

Look at the White Orientation Identity Chart and the Construction of Truth. A Fundamentalist is literal and fixed. It becomes very difficult to convince Fundamentalist teachers to use more right-brained lesson plans and to remove the pictures of White male U.S. presidents from their classroom walls.

Integrationists are willing to acknowledge that diverse opinions exist. Professor James Banks says that we no longer see the world from one (White) perspective but instead place the event in the center.

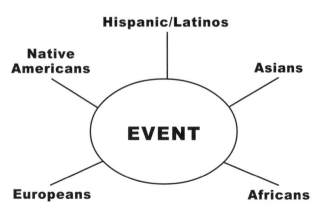

White Female Teachers

Someone with a literal and fixed perspective would only accept one position: Columbus discovered America. An Integrationist is willing to consider the Native American's perspective. It does not mean that an Integrationist believes other opinions, but they are willing to consider them.

The Transformationist, after a thorough analysis, might accept the view of others. A Transformationist, after listening to the Native American argument about whether Columbus discovered America, would acknowledge Native Americans to be the first people in America.

A teacher was lecturing to the students about the plight of Native Americans. She said, "We did not treat them very well." An African American student responded with disgust, "We? We? My people were slaves and had nothing to do with that!" In 1776 America adopted the Declaration of Independence that states, "All men are created equal." But it really only applied to White male property owners. Schools need to discuss the racist, sexist, and class implications.

Ana Maria Villegas and Tamora Lucas in the excellent book *Educating Culturally Responsive Teachers* recommend six strategies: 1. Gain social cultural consciousness; 2. Develop an affirming attitude toward students from culturally diverse backgrounds; 3. Develop the commitment and skills to act as agents of change; 4. Understand the transformist foundations of culturally responsive teaching; 5. Learn about students and their communities; and 6. Cultivate culturally responsive teaching practices.

The discussion of racism and race relations is a very sensitive subject. Why is it that I and a White consultant can say the same thing, but I'm ignored by some of the White staff? If Whites "don't see color," why is mine a factor? Do Whites assume

I will blame them for the achievement disparity? Do Whites receive an emotionally detached presentation better than one filled with passion? Maybe they feel threatened by me. Maybe they assume that I want them to quit their jobs so that African American students can have more teachers who look like them. However, anyone who has heard me speak will tell you that I'm equally demanding of African American teachers who are mis-educating African American students.

It is not my desire to remove White teachers, but I am concerned about schools that have a 50 percent or greater African American student population but less than 5 percent African American teaching staff. In spite of the above, as I said at the outset, the most important factor in improving academic achievement is not the race or gender of the teacher but her or his expectations and increasing "time on task." Fundamentalists want to hold to their hard-core beliefs that White children are smarter, their parents more involved, and all children can learn a Eurocentric curriculum with ditto sheets and textbooks.

One of the barometers I use to assess a staff's multicultural comfort level is their lesson plans and presentations on slavery. Often, liberal teachers will ask me, "When do you think we should teach African American children about slavery?" I cringe when I hear this question because it only appears that they are concerned about African American children. The reality is they are concerned about teaching a subject that they are in denial about. Jewish parents and educators teach their children about the Holocaust before age seven. We should take the same approach about slavery.

Schools don't teach the truth about Egypt, either. All children, Black and White, should know that the great Egyptian civilization was built by Africans and that Romans and Greeks had nothing to do with building pyramids, temples, and tombs.

White Female Teachers

This is very difficult for a Fundamentalist to swallow. It is challenging for an Integrationist. In addition to White authors Weiner, Howard, Teel, and Paley, I recommend the videotape from the *Oprah Winfrey Show* that featured Diane Elliot and her workshop on race relations.

A former schoolteacher, Ms. Elliot looks like a typical older White female teacher, but she's a warrior against racism. She forces other Whites to confront racism. In one of her exercises, she divided Whites in her audience into two groups based on eye color. Those with blue eyes were discriminated against. This show only lasted an hour, but within the hour Elliot created a society that helped Whites understand what Blacks endure on a daily basis. The blue-eyed group was frustrated, lacked unity, their self-esteem was depleted, and they were angry. It is often difficult for self-centered people to experience another person's pain and struggle.

One of the questions on the Multicultural Quiz concerned "good hair" and "pretty eyes." Unfortunately, many African American children and adults define good hair as long and straight and pretty eyes as any color but brown. Purposefully, Elliot discriminated against those with blue eyes. I have observed classrooms where African American children were stroking and combing the hair of their White female teacher. When I asked the teacher what she thought of that behavior, she was clueless. White teachers must encourage African American children to value their own hair, eyes, and hue.

White teachers have many different personalities. Thus far, we have discussed the concepts of denial, admitting, understanding, and appreciating and the postures of fundamentalist, integrationist, and transformationist. Further, some White teachers have a *missionary* complex. They believe they can "save" African American students. Missionaries believe people are "culturally deprived" if they do not possess the missionary's culture, Missionaries want to change the student's culture to be in accordance with their own. Can you save someone that you feel superior to? No. Could a missionary ever feel equal to the people he or she is trying to save? No. Will the victim always view the missionary with higher regard? Yes. Is missionary language condescending? Yes.

We also have the "liberal" teacher. They allow African American children to wear their hats in the school. They allow them to turn in inferior papers and reward them with unearned grades. They promote children to the next grade who have not satisfactorily performed. They think they are doing African Americans a favor because they feel that life has been too hard on them and lowering the standards will make life better.

Before Brown vs. Topeka (1954), many African American teachers and parents taught Rule 110. They taught their children that in a racist country, poor performance is unacceptable; therefore you must score 110. Jackie Robinson was taught as he entered major league baseball that a mediocre performance was unacceptable. Robinson knew he could not be an average baseball player. He had to be an all-star. One of the greatest problems that exist in our school systems is that very few African American children are being taught Rule 110. I appeal to every White teacher reading this chapter to incorporate this rule into their lessons.

Lisa Delpit describes condescension as "invisible racism." It is not overt but covert. Some White teachers provide less assistance to African American children. Others creatively find ways to avoid contact. African American children are not oblivious to this and respond with feelings of alienation, low morale, and unexpressed anger. Delpit writes that some White "liberal" educators feel that African American teachers are too authoritative, demanding, and harsh.[4]

In the excellent book *Because of The Kids* Karen Teel describes her transformation as a White teacher:
"I expected my students to:
1. Automatically pay attention to me when I talked
2. Listen to one another
3. Sit quietly in their seats when being spoken to
4. Raise their hands when they wanted to say something
5. Speak standard English
6. Speak politely
7. Follow my directions without complaint
8. Show respect toward me as the teacher."

When they did not do the above, she overlooked their bad behavior–call it fear, low expectations, racism, or all of the above. She later realized the children were testing her. She had to prove to them that as a White teacher she could control the class. When she became more assertive and demanding, viewing them as "her children," she earned their trust and respect.

The "insensitive" teacher can't put herself into another's place or empathize with another point of view. She may have only one Black student in her class, but because she has never experienced Black culture herself, she can't relate. One of the major reasons why many African American children do not seek advanced placement, honors, or gifted and talented classes is because African American children have major problems in those classes with insensitive teachers. These teachers attempt to make the only African American student the expert on all African American affairs. Whenever there is a Black issue being discussed, the insensitive teacher directs all eyes at the African American student.

White teachers should also read Russell Skiba's work. He released through Indiana University Press an excellent research document entitled *The Color of Discipline*. In this exhaustive study, he points out that it takes something major for White children to be suspended or expelled. They would have to be in possession of a knife or gun and there would have to be a serious injury. In contrast, if a White teacher only *felt* threatened by a Black male's look, body language, or clothing, the boy would be suspended or expelled. The former was objective and the latter was highly subjective.

Another way I attempt to evaluate a staff on racial sensitivity is to ask them how they feel observing four Black males in the school hallway. Do you feel differently when you see four White males in the hallway? What is the difference between a group and a gang? What is the difference between being assertive and aggressive? Why is it that so many groups of Black males are called gangs and considered aggressive while most White male congregations are considered groups and viewed as assertive?

Another popular personality in the White community is the "silent conspirator." This type says, "I didn't take your people from Africa. I'm working two jobs trying to make ends meet like everyone else." They say that they do not make derogatory comments about children and I believe them. The majority of White families in the nineteenth century did not own slaves in America. But just as it is naive for us to think that Adolph Hitler and not German apathy killed six million Jews, so is also naive to believe that a small percentage of White slaveholders maintained slavery by themselves.

White Female Teachers

In the teachers' lounge, only one out of ten teachers makes derogatory comments about the children. The remaining teachers do not make comments, but their silence condones the implications. Their lack of rebuttal fuels the conversation. Their silence confirms their beliefs.

A favorite race relations story of mine is about two college roommates, one African American and one White. They were very close in college, and both majored in business and had almost identical GPAs. They remained close after college and sought employment together. The African American was interviewed first by a White employer and was told that no positions were available. The White was interviewed by the same company and was hired. For months, the White roommate did not acknowledge he was racist. Although he did not make the hiring decision, he was a silent beneficiary of racism. In the criminal profession, they call that being an accomplice, and both parties are prosecuted. The future of African American children does not need to be in the hands of silent conspirators. I am reminded of White author Vivian Paley, who wrote *White Teacher*. She espouses that we should never just ignore racism in our schools.

I've worked with thousands of White teachers and I find that many want quick solutions. Dr. Barbara Sizemore, one of my mentors, taught me never to give a group your solutions without making sure there is a consensus on what caused the problem. Later I'll discuss solutions, but first we've got to address how to deal with White teachers who don't understand Black culture and Black children. If teachers believe that low-income, single-parent families cause poor academic performance, their expectations will be low. If teachers believe that the achievement gap is genetically driven, the solution of more right-brained lesson plans and a multicultural curriculum will not address the cause as they see it. If teachers believe that low funding equals low achievement, they will adjust their expectations accordingly.

In my book *Satan, I'm Taking Back My Health* I discuss how Americans of all colors, who eat fast food, want a pill to prevent heart disease, cancer, and diabetes. There are no quick fixes for White teachers who educate African American children. It will first require a change of attitude followed by a change of heart. Second, they will need to read about the African American experience. Third, they will need to take a walk through the community and listen to the residents. Remember the anecdote, "If you listen and observe children, they will teach you how to teach them."

On behalf of African American students, do you, as a White teacher, teach them because that is your desire? Do you teach them because you could not get hired at a White school? Are you teaching Black children while looking for a school with White children?

I have had the privilege of working with some of the best White educators of African American children in the country. There are large numbers of White teachers, male and female, who believe African Americans are excellent students. They have done what is necessary to bond with African American students. In my workshops, they sit in the front, ask questions, read books, and have African American students who perform above the national average. In the next chapter, we will look at African American teachers and evaluate their performance with African American students.

Chapter Three

African American Teachers

❖ Does the Black middle class live, work, spend, volunteer, or invest in the Black community?

This chapter is dedicated to my aunt and uncle Lucille and Bill Johnston who were teachers in Huntsville, Texas. They themselves were taught in one-room school shacks and were the products of Rule 110. Due to Jim Crow, many of our best Black minds were denied becoming engineers, accountants, computer programmers, and other professionals. Ironically, racism afforded African American students the opportunity to be educated by its best Black minds.

Once, my aunt and uncle told me that schools were becoming integrated and many White liberal teachers were giving African Americans unearned grades. They told me that they resented African American students trying to convince them that if they were truly Black, they should act like White liberal teachers. My relatives said that if being Black meant lowering the standards, you could call them Oreos or Uncle Toms for the rest of their lives because they were not going to compromise Rule 110.

This is the standard of excellence I would like African American educators to maintain. My teachers were 110 educators. They included Mrs. Avery, Mrs. Hudson, Mr. Payne, Mrs. Allen, Mrs. Butler, Mrs. Foote, Mrs. Marks, Mr. Boughton, Mrs. Talley, and Gerald Richards. These were some of the finest educators a student could have. I would pit these teachers against any in the country. It was an all-star lineup, but, unfortunately, it was a lineup created by segregation, racism, Jim Crow, and White supremacy.

Before Brown vs. Topeka and school integration, our best Black minds lived on the same block with those who had no degree. Children lived in the same neighborhoods with their teachers. They attended the same church and a "village" was created. In one of my earlier books, *Restoring the Village Solutions for the Family*, I go into far more detail about the village. Unfortunately, we not only have lost the village but our best Black minds are no longer majoring in education. What is more troubling, as I speak at about fifty colleges a year, is that when I ask African American students why they do not major in education, they tell me their parents, who are educators, told them not to major in education. It is a sad commentary when educators will not encourage their children to pursue their parents' field. Many youth tell me that they do not want to major in education because the children are too bad. Can you imagine a 19-year-old student trying to convince me that African American children are too bad? If they are too bad for African American college students, I wonder how White teachers feel about them?

The older generation of African American teachers saw their profession as a long-term commitment to African American children. Of the few African Americans who are pursuing education today, many of them see it as a transitional career step. They teach for three to five years before moving on to something more lucrative. When African Americans lost the village, there was a ripple effect throughout the Black community. Today, there is a widening gap between the Black haves and the Black have-nots. Twenty-five percent of African American households earn in excess of $50,000 a year. Yet 33 percent of African American households and 50 percent of its children live below the poverty line. The majority of African American teachers live in the suburbs but teach in the city. The majority of African

African American Teachers

American educators teach low-income African American children. It is rare for an African American teacher to live in the city and teach in the suburbs.

Many African Americans naively believed that when African Americans sat on the Supreme Court bench, became governor, senator, congressperson, mayor, superintendent of schools and police chief things were going to change. The first time an African American mayor is elected in a city, it feels like a revolution. But Blacks have made an error in judgment in thinking that Blacks in power would make their lives easier. As we've all discovered, unfortunately, Black skin doesn't always lead to positive change. In his book *The Mis-Education of the Negro* Carter G. Woodson asked, "educated to do what?" and educated to work for who?" He raised those questions in 1933, and they are just as significant nearly one hundred years later. No group of Africans in the world is better educated than African Americans. Two million have degrees and 1.5 million are attending college. But the question remains, educated to do what?

If my greatest challenge is providing in-service workshops for White teachers to close the achievement gap between White and Black students, then my second greatest challenge is when principals tell me classism is more significant than racism. An increasing number of middle-class African American teachers are lowering their expectations of low-income African American students. This is one of my major reasons for writing this book. The dynamics of race and class are strongly intertwined in the education of African American students. Some argue that if Black teachers lower their expectations for low-income African American students, it's not only classism but also racism. What is the difference between White or Black teachers if they both lower their expectations based on race?

How can an African American teacher suffer from amnesia so quickly? How can an African American teacher who was raised in the projects of the inner city now have such disdain for students who live there? How can African American teachers who split verbs just last night be so critical of students speaking Ebonics? How can African American teachers be so critical of African American males who look like their sons? Do African American educators teach African American students with the same zeal and determination that they teach their biological children? Do their biological children attend their school? Isn't it amazing that suburban African American teachers will send their children to schools where there are few, if any, African American teachers and yet in my workshop try to convince me that the problem is a shortage of African American teachers. If low-income African American children need African American teachers, don't middle-income African American children need them too?

What explains the achievement gap between White and Black students in Evanston, Illinois, Cleveland Heights, Ohio, Shaker Heights, Ohio, Ann Arbor, Michigan, Cambridge, Massachusetts, and similar cities? The Minority Student Achievement Network (MSAN) has been trying to answer this question. Why is the achievement gap wider among middle-class White and Black students versus lower-income White and Black students? What is the best environment for African American children? Inner city? Suburbs? Public schools? Private schools? African American teachers? White teachers?

When I was growing up in Chicago, there were numerous school strikes, but for some strange reason, my track coach would continue to conduct practice. He was paid only a small stipend when schools were in session, but it was obvious he was not in it for the money, and this was clearly evident during the school strike. He still required that we meet even if it had to be outside of the school grounds. I often asked him why he did that, and he said, "I don't want you to be behind when the season starts." I began to wonder where the African American math and reading teachers were, who, in spite of the school strike, could have organized us to have class in a church, library, community center, or their own house so that we would not fall behind in math and reading. It is a sad commentary that nationwide there are too many African American teachers who make decisions in the best interest of the union rather than African American children.

Please do not think that the only derogatory comments about African American children come from White teachers in the lounge. In many inner cities, schools have a predominately African American staff, but it does not mean that the content of the discussion in the lounge has changed or that academic achievement has been enhanced. In an earlier chapter, we described the IEP meeting that determines the placement of a child in special education. In many inner city schools there's a very good chance that there will be a high percentage of African American staff at the IEP, but it does not mean a reduction in African American students placed in special education.

Can you imagine what it is like for an African American educator who does not want to be Black but ends up in a low-income African American school, with students hanging out in the hallway, speaking Ebonics loudly? What is the appropriate response for the African American educator? What is the appropriate African American response when the White educator shakes her head and says, "That's the way these people are." Does the African American teacher concur with their White colleague? Does the African American educator just run and hide?

Do they like the fact that their White peers view them as being different, translated as "you are like one of us"? How can African American educators overcome class barriers and bond with African American students?

Educators could learn from Black colleges. How do Black colleges with only 16 percent of the total of African American students (the rest going to integrated schools) produce almost 30 percent of African American college graduates? How do Black colleges produce almost 75 percent of the African Americans who earn graduate degrees? How do Black colleges accept students that White colleges reject and produce graduates? What explains why White colleges that accept African Americans with higher GPAs and test scores have a lower graduation rate than Black colleges who accept lower-performing students? All educators need to appreciate–on the basis of the success of Black colleges–the importance of role models and bonding.

Where did Jesus meet the Samaritan woman? Did he meet her in Bethlehem? Did he meet her in Jerusalem? Or did he meet her in her neighborhood at the well? Why would Jesus, who could turn water into wine, walk on water, and calm a storm, ask a Samaritan for a cup of water? Likewise, how does Head Start turn a low-income, single, illiterate parent into a teacher's aide, teacher, and director? African American educators need to remember from whence they have come.

I will never forget when I was in sixth grade and Mrs. Butler asked me, "What is your math test score?" I said, "A hundred." When she asked me about my best friend, Darryl, I snickered. She asked me to bring my paper to her desk and she asked me again, "What was Darryl's grade?" I said, "Forty." She drew an X through my 100 and wrote 40 and said, "From now on, whatever grade Darryl receives will be yours." Mrs.

African American Teachers

Butler taught me more than math that year. She taught me values. "To whom much is given much is required, what you do unto the least of these you also do unto Me, blessed to be a blessing." There are more people of African descent in America with college degrees than any place in the world. There are more Africans in Nigeria, Ghana, South Africa, and Brazil, but there is no group better educated than African Americans. The future for African Americans should not be in the hands of educators who look like them but do not value or respect them. In the last chapter, we talked about those White teachers who have a missionary impulse toward African American children. That mind-set is better than that of an African American educator who is embarrassed and has disdain for African American students. Let me share with you some very interesting scholarship that, ironically, comes from a White professor, Thomas Dee of Swarthmore College. His article is titled "Teacher's Race and Student Achievement in Randomized Experiment."

> In brief the result of the test score evaluations indicate that exposure to an own race teacher did generate some substance of gain in student achievement for both Black and White students. More specifically these results suggest that a year with an own race teacher increased math and reading scores by 3-4 percentile points. Notably the estimated achievement gains associated with an own race teacher exist for nearly all groups of students defined by race, gender and several observed student, teacher and community characteristics. Overall, the results of this study provide evidence that ongoing efforts to recruit minority teachers are likely to be successful in generating improved outcomes for minority students.

The prior literature offers at least two general explanations why the racial pairing of students and teacher might exert an important influence on student achievement. These explanations are not mutually exclusive. One class of explanations involves what could be called passive teacher effect. These effects are triggered by the racial presence and not by explicit teacher behaviors. For example: one frequently cited reason for the relevance of a teacher's race is that by its mere presence the teacher's racial identity generates a sort of role model effect that engages student effort, confidence and enthusiasm. For example: it is possible for an underprivileged Black student in the presence of a Black teacher who encourages them to update their prior beliefs about the educational possibility. Similarly, students may feel more comfortable and focused in the presence of an own race regardless of the teacher's behavior. An alternative class of explanation for the educational benefits of own race teachers, points to active teacher effects. Race specific patterns of behavior among teachers including allocating class time and interacting with students and designing class materials, may indicate that teachers are more oriented toward students that share racial or ethnic background. For example: prior studies have indicated that Black students with White teachers receive less attention, are praised less, and scolded more than White counterparts.[5]

This very interesting research needs to be dissected and analyzed. On one hand, the importance of role modeling should

African American Teachers

be obvious. Can you be like anything that you have not seen? In my book *Countering the Conspiracy to Destroy Black Boys* I advocate for more Black male teachers. I am very concerned about the large number of schools where there's not one Black man in the building, and if the man is present, he is probably a custodian, security guard, PE teacher, or principal, not a classroom teacher. There are African American children who have gone from kindergarten through sixth grade and have not experienced an African American male teacher. I also mentioned CIBI, a network of Africentric schools that advocates for more African American teachers. Because of Jim Crow legislation, 80 percent of my teachers were African American. Black children benefited from these teachers. My aunt and uncle are prime evidence that the research of Dr. Dee was correct.

We know quantitatively that if African American students have Black teachers for one year, they improve 4 percentage points in reading and math. This research cannot be ignored. Can you imagine the results if African American students had several consecutive years of African American teachers, especially in the primary grades? African American educators must realize their own significance to the children in our community. The government must realize their significance and do what is necessary financially to increase the number of African American educators.

But how do we reconcile Dee's research with my position, that it's not about race or gender of the teacher but about setting high expectations? How do I utilize Dee's research when 93 percent of America's teachers are non-African American? It is one thing for me to promote African American teachers, but that's like a coach reminiscing about the good old days when he had an all-star lineup. The reality is we must win today with our current players. How do I evaluate Dee's research when African American teachers do not encourage their children to pursue education? How do I integrate Dee's research when some African American educators have a disdain for African American students and don't see teaching as a lifetime commitment? How do I encourage White educators who read this research and conclude there's really nothing they can do for African American students because they're White?

I believe it's possible to accept Dee's research and still hold that setting high expectations and requiring that more of a teacher's time be spent on task are key to enhancing student performance. There is a difference between teaching and role modeling. Many times when I work with White teachers nationwide, they wonder if I am going to recommend that they quit their jobs and be replaced with Black staff. Instead, I encourage them to raise their expectations and invite African American role models on a weekly basis to talk with their students. All children need role models, and a component of Dee's research encompasses the importance of role modeling for the long-term development of the child.

I also recommend that every African American with a degree consider teaching at least one year in a public school. Of all the things I've done in my career, the most rewarding, other than preaching, has been inspiring almost a thousand African American males to become teachers, most of them at the fourth-grade level.

On behalf of African American students, be honest with yourself: Do you teach them because that is your desire? Would you prefer teaching where you live? Is it your desire to teach where your children attend?

In the next chapter, "Master Teachers," I'll address what students need from teachers regardless of the teacher's race or income.

Chapter Four

Master Teachers

- ❖ The most significant characteristic of Master Teachers is not their race or gender but the expectations they have of their students.
- ❖ Students need teachers who will make them learn.
- ❖ A multicultural teacher must have multicultural values.
- ❖ Teach on your feet, not in your seat.
- ❖ If you listen and observe children, they will tell you how to teach them.
- ❖ It's a teacher's job to inspire students–especially if they lack the motivation to learn.
- ❖ Telling is not teaching.
- ❖ I don't become what I think I can, I don't become what you think I can, I become what I think you think I can.
- ❖ Understand the difficulties your students have in the community and at home, but refuse to victimize them further by making excuses for them in the classroom.
- ❖ If a student has not learned, the educator has not taught.
- ❖ No significant learning occurs without a significant relationship.
- ❖ The mediocre teacher tells. The good teacher explains. The superior teacher demonstrates. The great teacher inspires.
- ❖ Effective teachers use a relevant curriculum that involves critical thinking, and pedagogy that will produce tomorrow's leaders.
- ❖ You can't teach what you don't care about to people you don't care about.

❖ In the ideal classroom, teachers and students listen to each other and work together on real problems. Teachers become facilitators and students discover answers.

Several years ago, a newspaper researched a group of successful people from one community. In seeking to find out why they had succeeded, it turned out that they all had the same kindergarten teacher 40 years earlier. She had instilled in each of them a love of learning and a feeling of competence that made them eager to meet new challenges. This one teacher's effort impacted her students, their families, and the community decades later.

This may very well be the most important chapter in the book. In order for us to successfully educate African American children, we must understand the characteristics of Master Teachers. We must develop more Master Teachers and ensure that they are in schools populated by African American children. The following observations in this chapter come as a result of having been a former classroom teacher and educator for almost thirty years and having read hundreds of books on this subject.

Lisa Delpit, in her book *Other People's Children*, was told by a 12-year-old friend that there are three types of teachers. First there are Black teachers, none of whom are afraid of Black kids–who "don't play that." Second, White teachers, the majority of whom are afraid of Black kids. And third, the remaining few White teachers who are not afraid of Black kids.[6]

Gloria Ladson-Billings in her book *Dreamkeepers*, along with the research of L. Winfield, describes six types of teachers. The first are "Custodians." These teachers do not believe that much can be done to help their students and do not look to others to help them maintain classes. The second group is "Referral

Agents." They also do not believe that much can be done to help their students improve, but they shift the responsibility to other school personnel by sending children the school psychologist or the special education teacher. "Tutors" believe that students can improve and they believe that it is their responsibility to help them do so. "General Contractors" also believe that improvement is possible, but they look for ancillary personnel, aides, resource teachers, and others to provide academic assistance rather than take on the responsibility themselves. "Conductors" believe that students are capable of excellence, and they assume responsibility for ensuring their students achieve that excellence. The last group is "Coaches." They also believe that their students are capable of excellence, but they are comfortable sharing the responsibility of helping them achieve with parents, community members, and the students.[7]

In my work, I have observed five types of teachers. First, Custodians who spend large amounts of time in the teachers' lounge and do not believe that African American children can learn. They believe that the major hindrances are social demographics and a child's home life. Often, Custodians are nearing retirement and love using the classic phrase, "I have mine, you have to get yours." They are quick to remind you that they have two years, four months, three weeks, four days, three hours, and seventeen minutes before retirement. Custodians are known to use the same lesson plans over a 30-year period.

Like Ladson-Billings, I have also observed Referral Agents. Many principals have told me that 20 percent of staff generates almost 80 percent of the referrals for special education and suspension. This is why I implore principals and superintendents to make my workshops mandatory. If staff meetings are voluntary and optional, Custodians and Referral

Agents won't come in unless they are paid. These same people are critical of schools that pay parents to attend meetings. Isn't it also interesting that when an African American student is with a Master Teacher he or she has less of a chance of being referred to special education? Unfortunately, Custodians and Referral Agents have unions and African American children do not. Therefore, Referral Agents continue their behavior and African American children suffer.

The third group is Instructors; they believe they teach subjects, not children. They are quick to tell me *what* they teach rather than *whom* or *how* they teach. They don't believe in developing self-esteem, nurturing, or right-brain learning theories. We have a greater number of Instructors after third grade. How unfortunate that when the scores of African American children begin to decline, we have an increasing number of Instructors. In a subsequent chapter on African American students, we will provide more details and theories on the importance of bonding. Unfortunately, there is very little bonding between students and Instructors.

The fourth group is Teachers. They understand the significance of subject matter, but they also believe that you shouldn't teach the most comfortable way, but the way children learn. Therefore, if you have a greater percentage of right-brained thinkers, you should increase the percentage of right-brained lesson plans. These students are holistic learners and look for a larger meaning. They prefer cooperative learning, and can learn with a higher noise level and greater movement. Their strengths lie in music, art, and physical activities.

My last group is Coaches, who understand subject matter and pedagogy but also understand the need to bond with students first. Coaches care, respect, and appreciate the culture of their students. They fully understand that there can be no significant learning until there is a significant relationship. Author and professor Peter Murrell, Jr., calls these people "community teachers." Scholar and policy-maker Martin Haberman penned the book *Star Teachers of Children in Poverty.* Coaches understand the child and their neighborhood and provide complementary curriculum and pedagogy. They are less concerned about discipline and order and more concerned about creating lesson plans that excite and engage students. Star Teachers, in Haberman's terminology, convince students that effort is more important than ability.

Let's recap:

1. Delpit
   a. Black teachers unafraid
   b. White teachers afraid
   c. White teachers unafraid

2. Ladson-Billings
   a. Custodians
   b. Referral Agents
   c. Tutors
   d. General Contractors
   e. Conductors
   f. Coaches

3. Kunjufu
   a. Custodians
   b. Referral Agents
   c. Instructors
   d. Teachers
   e. Coaches

I have noticed that in low-achieving schools, the most negative room in the school is not the classroom but the teachers' lounge. Most Master Teachers tell me that they spend very little time in the teachers' lounge. Instead, they use free time to develop new lesson plans, grade papers, read additional books, and try to improve their craft.

If you've ever sat in the teachers' lounge when the discussion turns to the lack of performance of African American students, you will hear causes propounded that include income status, fatherlessness, and genetics. Unfortunately, there are educators who believe Charles Murray's theories, expounded in and his book *The Bell Curve*. Many believe that African American children are genetically inferior to White children. Isn't it ironic that the causes put forward by Custodians, Referral Agents, and Instructors are outside their sphere of influence. There is nothing an educator can do about income, fatherlessness, and genetics.

Can a teacher improve the income status of the family? Let us not forget that African American median income is only 61 percent of White income. Should African American children and their parents be blamed for institutional racism? Ironically, 61 percent of income is almost equivalent to three-fifths of a person? Can a teacher reduce the divorce rate and the lack of involvement of the father in the home? It is also amazing to me that the divorce rate in the teaching profession is not much better. The national divorce rate is 50 percent but 66 percent for African Americans. Can teachers change the racial make-up of their student?

If you know that African American children need more attention because of lack of income and fatherlessness, then why not increase your effort, set higher expectations, and devote more time on task to circumvent these causes? I challenge Custodians,

Referral Agents, and Instructors to re-think their approach to teaching Black children.

A study done by the Education Trust called "Good Teaching Matters" found that there was an 89 percent pass rate on the Texas state assessment by the Loma Terrace School in El Paso. The Mission Independent School District in Texas with a 94 percent poverty rate reports a 95 pass rate for their fourth graders. The Second Community School District in New York continues to outperform other school districts in spite of their high poverty rate.[8]

The harmful effects of a poor teacher can linger well into the future, and a string of bad teachers can leave students at a huge academic disadvantage, researchers at the University of Tennessee, Knoxville, have concluded. Their study is based on an analysis of scores from the Tennessee Comprehensive Assessment Program, which measures performance in math, reading, language arts, science, and social studies each year in grades two through eight. William Sanders, a professor, statistician, and the leader of the research team, predicted how much a student should improve on the test each year based on that pupil's previous scores. The following graphs show the results of this approach.

The Effect of Different Teachers On
Low-Achieving Students
Tennessee

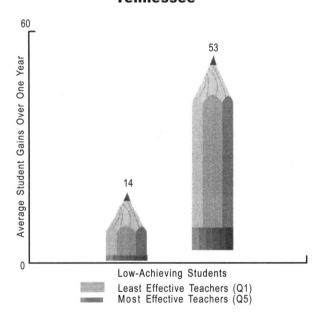

Sanders, William L. and Rivers, Joan C. "Cumulative And Residual Effects of Teachers on Future Student Academic Achievement."

Master Teachers

Cumulative Effects of Teacher Sequence on Fifth Grade Math Scores: Tennessee

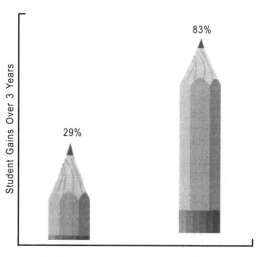

Student Gains Over 3 Years

29%

83%

Students With 3 Very
Ineffective Teachers

Students With 3 Very
Effective Teachers

Sanders, William L. and Rivers, Joan C. "Cumulative And Residual Effects of
Teachers on Future Student Academic Achievement."

51

Effects On Students' Reading
Scores In Dallas (Grades 4-6)

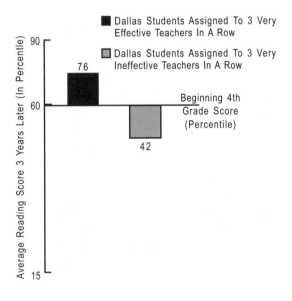

Source: Heather Jordan, Robert Mendro, & Dash Weerasinghe,
"Teacher Effects On Longitudinal Student Achievement" 1997.

Master Teachers

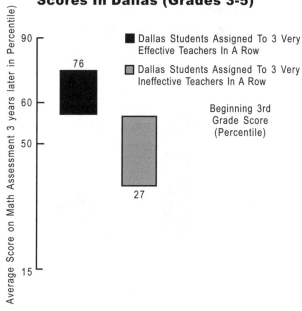

Effects On Students' Math Scores In Dallas (Grades 3-5)

Average Score on Math Assessment 3 years later in Percentile)

90

76

60

50

15

■ Dallas Students Assigned To 3 Very Effective Teachers In A Row

☐ Dallas Students Assigned To 3 Very Ineffective Teachers In A Row

Beginning 3rd Grade Score (Percentile)

27

Source: Heather Jordan, Robert Mendro, & Dash Weerasinghe, "Teacher Effects On Longitudinal Student Achievement" 1997.

Boston Students With Effective
Teachers Showed Greater Gains

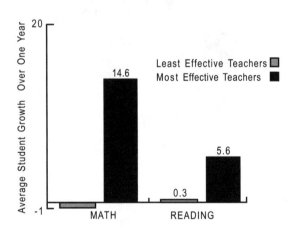

Source: Boston Public Schools, "High School Restructuring,"
March 9, 1998.

Master Teachers

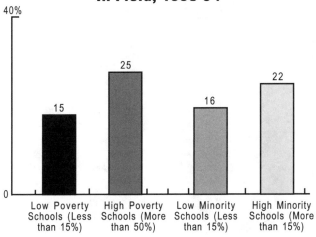

**Percentage of Classes Taught By
Teachers Lacking A Major
In Field, 1993-94**

- Low Poverty Schools (Less than 15%): 15
- High Poverty Schools (More than 50%): 25
- Low Minority Schools (Less than 15%): 16
- High Minority Schools (More than 15%): 22

Source: Richard Ingersoll, University of Georgia, Unpublished, 1998.

African American Students Are More Likely To Have Underqualified Teachers: Tennessee

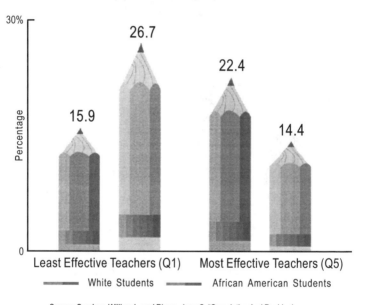

Source: Sanders, William L. and Rivers, Joan C. "Cumulative And Residual Effects of Teachers on Future Student Academic Achievement."

Master Teachers

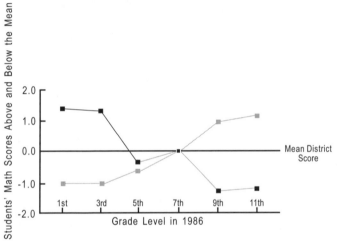

Long-Range Effects
Of Low-Scoring and High-Scoring Teachers
On Student Achievement (Texas)

Students' Math Scores Above and Below the Mean

2.0

1.0

0.0 — Mean District Score

-1.0

-2.0

1st   3rd   5th   7th   9th   11th

Grade Level in 1986

—■— Districts with Low-Scoring 1st and 3rd Graders and High-Scoring Teachers
—■— Districts with High Scoring 1st and 3rd Graders and Low-Scoring Teachers

Source: Ronald F. Ferguson, "Evidence That Schools Can Narrow
the Black-White Test Score Gap," 1997.

Sanders and his colleagues analyzed the math scores of students in two districts. They found that groups of students with comparable achievement levels in grade two had vastly different test scores by grade five and that their scores were strongly correlated with the quality of their teachers. Quality was defined based on the teacher's college grade point average, major in college, passing the state certification exam, and past academic track record with students. Fifth graders who spent three years with teachers deemed ineffective averaged 54 to 60 percentile points lower than students who had a series of highly effective teachers. The effects of even one bad or good teacher were still reflected in the test scores two years later.

Researchers in the Dallas School District have shown that having a less effective teacher can significantly lower a student's performance over time, even if the student has more competent teachers later. Evidence that students of good teachers tend to perform better might not seem surprising, but district officials were struck by just how much teacher quality mattered to student achievement. Building on the work of researcher William Sanders in Tennessee, Dallas researchers started by dividing about 1,500 of the district's 8,500 teachers, those for whom complete personnel records were available, into five groups of equal size, from least to most effective.

Teacher effectiveness was based on comparisons of the test results of students with similar backgrounds. Teachers whose students made the greatest gains on the assessments, which included the Iowa Test of Basic Skills (ITBS) and the state test, were deemed most effective. The researchers also took into account student background factors, such as race, ethnicity, English proficiency, and poverty.

The researchers tracked the three-year progress of about 17,000 students in grades four through eight. Students who had the most effective teachers generally made far greater gains on the ITBS than those who had mostly less effective teachers. For example, the average reading scores of a group of sixth graders who had three of the most effective teachers in a row rose from just under the 60th percentile to about the 75th percentile. A similar group of students who had two of the least effective teachers and then one of the most effective ones dropped from just above the 60th percentile to just below the 50th percentile.

A study in North Carolina suggested that a 1 percent decrease in teachers' scores on the National Teachers Exam (NTE) would bring about a 5 percent relative decline in the percentage of students who pass standardized competency exams. The research notes that the percentages of classes taught by teachers who do not have a major in the subject they are teaching is far greater in high-poverty, high-minority schools than in low-poverty and low-minority schools. There are middle schools, junior high schools, and high schools with teachers who are assigned to teach math and science but did not major in either of those subjects. It is estimated that 25 percent of inner-city teachers are unqualified to teach the subjects they are instructing.

Thirty-one percent of New York City teachers initially failed the state exam while only 4 percent of teachers in the affluent White suburbs failed the exam. Unfortunately, African American children live primarily in the city. In Chicago one of ten teachers fails the exam. In California, 20 percent (58,000) teachers failed the exam. Ironically, failing teachers in the city are allowed to continue to teach, some indefinitely. These teachers would be removed in affluent White suburbs, but because our society has low expectations for urban African American youth, they are permitted to remain in the city schools.

In Milwaukee a student sneaked a video recorder into school and taped a teacher reading a newspaper while students were shooting craps in the back of the room. The video was aired on television, and superintendent Howard Fuller demanded the teacher's termination. The union prevailed and the teacher never lost any income or her job. Another teacher placed a dunce cap on the head of a 13-year-old mentally retarded boy and led students in throwing objects at the boy. The teacher was suspended for 30 days and then transferred. Lastly, one teacher punished a fifth-grade boy for fighting by plunging the boy's head into a toilet filled with urine and feces and would not allow him to clean his head before boarding the bus. The teacher was suspended for 81 days and then transferred.

Many principals have told me that recruiting good teachers requires will, time, and tenacity. Others have said, "It requires an act of God to remove a teacher." In Milwaukee not one of 6,000 teachers between 1985 and 1990 were fired for poor teaching and not one of 1,000 teachers were denied tenure. This is further exacerbated by a teacher shortage, which is acute in the inner city, particularly in high school math and science departments.[9]

Do we have enough effective teachers for all students? If not, what leverage do principals have to hold less qualified teachers accountable and improve their performance? Is the problem teacher shortage or teacher retention? One-third of new teachers quit within three years and 50 percent leave after five years. We want teachers to act like professionals, but few school districts provide adequate teacher training and mentoring. Saturn automobile workers receive 92 hours annually of training to produce a car, while teachers receive less than 25 hours to develop a child.

Master Teachers

Every new teacher needs to be mentored by a master teacher for a minimum of three years. New teachers should be given time to observe master teachers in the classroom and vice versa. Linda Darling-Hammond documents in her excellent book *The Right to Learn* that when school districts make professional development the priority, they can find auxiliary staff and scheduling opportunities, which allow teachers time to develop. Student achievement increased when New York City's Community District 2 made professional development the priority. In Japan, teachers collaboratively develop, review, and evaluate lesson plans. They have systemized lesson plan development, therefore there is less variance in Japanese classrooms in contrast to the United States.

In the thought provoking book *The Teaching Gap* by James Stigler and James Hiebert, they contrast the teaching styles of American and Japanese teachers. In America, teachers give facts and students memorize. They give problems, procedures, and formulas, and students must work harder to solve problems. In American schools, students struggle less with problems while in Japan, teachers feel students will develop critical thinking skills and master the concept, if they discover for themselves the proper formula to solve problems.

I am very concerned with the academic achievement gap, but it is more acute in math at the upper grade level. I have observed schools where there is a 50 percent differential between reading and math scores I am now spending an equal amount of consulting time between improving academics of African American males and enhancing math scores. I encourage educators to read *Radical Equations* by Robert Moses, *Twice As Less* by Eleanor Orr, *The Teaching Gap* by James Stigler and James Hiebert, *How to Teach Math to Black Students* by Shahid

Muhammad, and the research of the Benjamin Banneker Association. This math achievement gap explains why 86 percent of the NBA is African American, but less than 2 percent of the engineers, doctors, computer programmers, and accountants. We must shatter the African American psyche that they are better in music than math.

In the final chapter, Models of Success, I will look at policy implications from "Good Teaching Matters." I hope teachers in the lounge will discuss this matter. The problem is not that the children are low income, fatherless, and possess more melanin than others, but that their teacher's college GPA, test scores on the NTE, college major, and past teaching performance were not up to standards. In reviewing the graphs, notice that the test scores of White affluent children declined, in spite of their race, income, and parental status, when subjected to three years of ineffective teaching. In contrast, the graphs also show that the scores of low-income African American children improved after receiving several years of effective teaching.

This reminds me of my disdain for Ward Connerly and his desire to abolish affirmative action nationwide. There were hundreds of African American students in the state of California in 2000 who scored 1200 or better on the SAT and had a 4.0 GPA but were denied admission to the University of California, Berkeley, because they were beaten out by students who had close to a 5.0 GPA. This occurred because advanced placement grades are "weighted higher." A "C" in advanced placement is valued as a "B" in regular classes and the "A" in advanced placement is viewed as a 5.0 rather than a 4.0 as in regular classes. How could African American students in low-income schools compete against affluent White suburbanites when their low-income school probably offered very few if any AP classes? They were denied admission not because they were at-risk but because their schools were at-risk and they had no opportunity to gain a 5.0 GPA. A school is at-risk by the way, if it has any of the following characteristics: ineffective administrators and teachers, poor time on task, unqualified teachers, an irrelevant Eurocentric curriculum, a disproportionate percentage of left-brain lesson plans, tracking, and negative peer pressure.

In my work with Master Teachers and Coaches, I have observed that they:

- Are enthusiastic about discussing course material.
- Speak clearly, understandably and calmly.
- Have voices that are clear and understandable.
- Listen to students and apologize when in error.
- Never intimidate or embarrass students.
- Use student questions as a source for discovering points of confusion.
- Are readily available for consultation with students.
- Treat all students with respect and assign room captains .
- Return assignments in a reasonable time.
- Slow down when discussing complex and difficult topics.
- Are consistently well prepared and organized for class.
- Are aware of what material has been covered in previous classes.
- Are well prepared to answer questions.
- Dress professionally.
- Subscribe to educational journals.
- Enroll in classes to improve their craft.
- Reserve an area for tardy and unruly students.

I love observing Coaches. One of the consistent traits I've observed in Coaches is that they delay going to the textbook until a bond has been established with students. In contrast, on the very first day of school Custodians, Referral Agents, and Instructors quickly utilize the textbook and ditto sheets. From a Coach's vantage point, this is a cardinal sin. You don't teach children until you bond. Significant learning cannot take place until a significant relationship has been established. Coaches are very clear on this virtue. They also believe that you cannot teach a child that you do not love, respect, and understand. If you can't appreciate a child's culture, you can't appreciate or teach the child. Children know when you love them and when you don't. Children know when you respect them and when you don't.

In the chapter on White Female Teachers, I discussed the "showdown." Master Teachers do not lose showdowns. The beauty of Coaches is that their students seldom challenge them because they have bonded. During the critical first week of the school year, Master Teachers establish the fact that they are the mother or father of the classroom and the students are their children. They establish clear rules, which are visibly posted like the Ten Commandments. During the first week, the rules are clearly explained and students understand the consequences of breaking them. A miniature contract is established. The students are taught to believe that they are brothers and sisters. Many Custodians, Referral Agents, and Instructors spend a disproportionate percentage of time disciplining students. Master Teachers spend less time disciplining students because they have instilled in the children the idea that they are a family.

In one of my earlier books, *Developing Positive Self Images and Discipline in Black Children,* I describe in detail "Unity Criticism Unity."[10] This is a session somewhat like family time, wherein the Coach allocates five to ten minutes per day for students to resolve conflicts with each other. The teacher first asks the children if they have any compliments they want to share with each other. Children need to be taught to see the good in each other. Then, if the students have a problem with someone, they can raise their hand. Raising their hands, being orderly and respectful, is important. The child being criticized cannot respond. We must teach children to develop self-control and avoid reacting impetuously. The fourth time around the room, the children being criticized can respond. Upon completion of the dialogue, the Coach (judge) asks the students (jury) for the verdicts and punishments. The Coach provides a list of punishments to the jury. The session concludes with additional compliments or chants. We start in unity, have criticism, and end in unity.

When students don't perform, Coaches will look them in the eye and say, "You really disappointed me." Custodians, Referral Agents, and Instructors could not use that statement with the same effect as Coaches because there was no bonding. Coaches can use this statement as a powerful tool to develop and shape the behavior of their students. *I don't become what I think I can, I don't become what you think I can, I become what I think you think I can.*

In my 30-year career as an education consultant, I have worked with teachers on setting expectations. I believe that what you see in the child will be what you produce from the child. I often stand before an audience of teachers and show them a picture of a dark-skinned African American male and ask them, "What do you see in this child? Do you see a drug dealer or a dentist? Do you see a computer programmer or a convict?" Whatever you see in the child will be what you produce from the child. How telling that many kindergarten through third grade teachers see African American children as cute, but many fourth through twelfth grade teachers become very intimidated.

Many of you have heard the story of an Instructor who was frustrated because he was given a challenging group of students. The Instructor felt that the principal had been unfair, and one day, while the principal was out of his office, she snuck into the office and reviewed the children's IQ scores. The Instructor just assumed that they would be low. The Instructor was startled to see the IQ scores: 118, 120, 122, 124, 126, etc. The Instructor had made a critical mistake. For half the school year, she had lowered her expectations because she felt that her students' poor behavior meant that they weren't smart. Now, realizing that these children were brilliant and gifted with high IQs, the Instructor proceeded for the remainder of the school year to raise expectations. The class out-performed the other classrooms in the school and received many accolades for their performance. The Instructor felt guilty and just had to share the story with the principal. The principal made the Instructor promise that she would never sneak into the office again, but shared the fact with the Instructor that those were not IQ scores but locker room numbers! The implications of that story resonate throughout America, where Custodians, Referral Agents, and Instructors literally destroy the education potential of African American children.

Over the years, I've been a strong advocate of TESA (Teacher Expectations Student Achievement), which is now GESA (Gender Expectations Student Achievements). When I first became an educational consultant, I would ask educators, "Do you believe all children learn?" My audience would give me a resounding "Yes." But over the years, I have noticed that not all teachers believe that all children can learn and that their expectations can be quantitatively measured. It is not enough to say that all children can learn when we don't see evidence of that in the classroom.

Master Teachers

One of the ways that GESA measures expectations is by noting students' opportunities to respond. Master Teachers provide an equitable distribution of students' response opportunities. Many Custodians, Referral Agents, and Instructors have bad habits and are not comfortable being observed and video taped. They offer an unequal distribution of response opportunities. They call on some students far more than they call on others. It is possible that they are unaware of this bad habit, but students are very much aware of the disparity. African American males are very cognizant that girls are recognized more frequently.

Another evaluation instrument that GESA uses is feedback and reinforcement. Master teachers engage all of their students equally. They ask a student a question and if the student answers incorrectly, the teacher engages the student and provides additional clues to help the student provide the correct answer. Research shows that low-achieving African American males have about six seconds to correct a wrong answer. In contrast, high-achieving females are given more than three minutes to change a wrong answer. This is reinforced by editors Christopher Jencks and Meredith Phillips in their excellent book *The Black-White Test Score Gap*. Why would a teacher engage a child for three minutes if she did not expect the correct answer to be forthcoming? It is not enough for teachers to say that all children can learn when there is an unequal distribution of response opportunities and students are engaged differently.

One of the strategies that Coaches use to ensure equal distribution of response opportunities is to set up a box containing all the students' names; they simply take out a random name and call upon that student. When the box is empty, they put all the names back into the box. Master Teachers also find ways to smile, give a word of encouragement, and stand equally close to all of their students. Conversely, we have observed teachers who throughout the entire day are never physically close to certain students. They never provide a hug, smile, or word of encouragement.

There is a science to where children sit in class. It is no accident that lower-achieving students sit either off to the side or in the rear. I have witnessed tragic stories where the girls are in front, and the boys are in the rear; White children are in the front, and African American children are in the rear; or light-skinned children are in the front and dark-skinned children are in the rear. This discrimination does not go unnoticed by African American students.

What separates the Master Teachers from the Instructors, Custodians, and Referral Agents? Master Teachers set high expectations while the others do not. The following are only a few of the reasons why some teachers expect so little of their students:

1. Gender – lower expectations for elementary boys and for older girls. This stems from research that boys mature slower.

2. Income and education – lower expectations due to income, employment, and educational status.

3. Race – lower expectations for minority status.

4. Test scores, permanent records – belief in fixed ability preclude possibility of improvement and higher expectations.

5. Negative comments about students – lounge talk, other teachers or principal's evaluations result in lower expectations.

6. Type of school – rural and inner city schools are associated with lower expectations.

7. Appearance – lower expectations associated with clothes or grooming that are out of style, cheaper material, etc.

8. Oral language patterns – negative cues from any non-standard English result in lower expectations.

9. Neatness – lower expectations associated with general disorganization, poor handwriting, etc.

10. Halo effect – tendency to label a child's overall ability based on one characteristic. Poor behavior becomes the basis of overall negative evaluation.

11. Readiness – assuming that maturation rates or prior lack of knowledge or experience preclude improvement.

12. Socialization – experienced teachers' tendency to stress limitations on students.

13. Student behavior – lower academic expectations for students with poor behavior.

14. Teacher training institutions – perpetuate myths and ideologies of individual limitations.

15. Tracking – labeling and accentuating differences among students result in lower expectations.

16. Seating position – lower expectations for sides and backs of classrooms.[11]

Madeline Hunter, in her excellent book *Mastery Teaching*, believes that the success of students lies in the hands of educators. She believes that there are two major issues. The first is the level of difficulty of the learning task. Remember, school is the first place where children learn to fail. We can change that paradigm by no longer believing that all 30 children are at the same level and acknowledge that even within the same grade there are different levels of achievement. Madeline Hunter suggests that we can adjust the difficulty level of the task being presented to a student. The second factor is that teaching skill will determine student outcome. She reinforces the research of the Education Trust and "Good Teaching Matters."

Peter Murrell, Jr., writes in *African Centered Pedagogy* that accomplished teachers of African American children create an intellectual and cultural environment that stimulates learning. They understand and appreciate African American culture, history, and language and continue to study to learn more. Accomplished teachers of African American children understand the distinction between training and educating and choose the latter. Their desire is to produce academically sound, compassionate, Africentric students who can cope successfully in a Eurocentric society.

In my work with school districts, I always stress raising expectations and increasing time on task. What Charles Murray failed to mention in the *Bell Curve* is that the major reason for the achievement gap is not income, parental involvement, or genetics, but time on task. Asians in high school study 12 hours per week, White students study 8 hours per week, while African

Master Teachers

Americans study only 4 hours per week. Ineffective teachers feel vindicated when I document African American students' sparse study time and their 30 hours of television viewing, 18 hours of rap music, 11 hours on the telephone, and 9 hours outside playing.

In a later chapter, we will look at what parents can do to correct this abysmal behavior. But for now, we have to ask ourselves how we can improve time management in the classroom. Let's not deceive ourselves by thinking that every teacher in the building is providing the same number of hours for instruction. In the lowest achieving school in the city, there is always at least one teacher who has his or her children above the national average. I then challenge teachers by asking them, "Do you want to look at 29 failures or do you want to look at 1 success story?"

How do Master Teachers make success stories of low-income and fatherless children? First, they set high expectations. Second, they spend the greatest number of minutes on instruction. In the typical nine to three o'clock school day, minus lunch, theoretically we have approximately five hours for instruction. But if a teacher loses five minutes a day, multiplied by five days in a week, multiplied by 10 months in a school year, he or she has lost four weeks of instruction!

How do ineffective teachers lose five minutes per day? Many Custodians, Referral Agents, and Instructors read their newspapers, balance their checkbooks, cut out food coupons, surf the Web, return e-mail, talk to their colleagues across the hall, and spend more time disciplining children than educating them. They allow students to waste their time when materials are missing. In contrast, Master Teachers have a central location in their room with extra pencils, pens, crayons, scissors, paper, and books because they refuse to cater to irresponsible behavior. In low-achieving schools teachers are interrupted 25 times daily by administration concerns. In Japan, class time is considered sacred and interruptions are not allowed.

Master Teachers are very much aware that the first and last five minutes of the class are the most important. Madeline Hunter calls this "primetime."[12] Custodians, Referral Agents, and Instructors will be found taking attendance, making announcements, waiting for students to straggle in, disciplining students, reviewing their lesson plans, and passing out materials—all activities that Madeline Hunter describes as "soap opera activities." In contrast, a Coach's lesson plan is on the chalkboard before students walk through the door. He or she is ready to begin teaching the first five minutes. Ineffective teachers are more concerned about behavior management while Coaches are more concerned about bonding and intellectually challenging students. The latter eliminates or greatly reduces behavioral problems.

There are a couple of things teachers can do to get class started right away. Begin by discussing "This Day in Black History." This will stretch Black history through the entire year (beyond February) and will put students in the right mind-set to learn. Master Teachers find ways to teach Black history every day of the school year. Second, I recommend a daily word problem. African American youth must become skilled at critical thinking. Many youth understand basic math functions but do not know how to apply them in word problems. Teachers can also use "brain twisters" and problems of logic.

In my observations of African American students, and particularly right-brained learners, I have noticed that many of them need additional time before they begin the task. Right-brained thinkers need to "set the stage." Their desk needs to be just right, their pencil needs to be sharpened a certain way, or they need to look around to see the status of their peers. I've observed many of my employees who need to set the stage, and this concerns me within the context of time on task because I understand the importance of the first five minutes. My recommendation to teachers is to continue to demand time on task during the first five minutes, but allow some students, who you know will perform well, a few more seconds to set their stage.

In an in-service workshop a teacher once asked me, "How many seconds or minutes are acceptable?" Many right-brained students, who have the ability to perform well, unfortunately spend their day in the corner or the principal's office because their teachers failed to recognize their need to "set the stage." I suggest a maximum of four minutes. Interestingly, these students are oftentimes found still working after the period has ended! They simply needed flexibility in the beginning.

Here's a typical scenario. In one classroom we have a student who is a fast learner. He or she is given 30 problems to answer in 60 minutes. The student completes the problems in 30 minutes. Unfortunately, because the teacher lacks good classroom management and time on task skills, the student is not given anything else to do for the remaining 30 minutes. So he pulls Diane's hair, throws spitballs across the room, talks to friends, and is sent to the corner or to the principal's office. There is a thin line determining whether African American children are placed in gifted and talented or behavior disorder classrooms.

We have one student who needs to "set the stage" and another who completes the work in half the time. We have 5 percent of students who create 90 percent of the disciplinary problems and want to be involved in a "showdown." How many teachers are prepared in college education departments for a student who needs to "set the stage," a fast learner, and a "showdown"? Yet all this can take place in one class period, 90 percent in the first and last 5 minutes by five percent of the students. I call this Rule 555.

Master Teachers normally arrive an hour early, stay an hour late, and do not spend time in the teachers' lounge. Conversely, the majority of the people in the teachers' lounge arrive just in time to teach and leave with the students when the bell rings. Master Teachers not only arrive early and stay late but students become aware of their schedule and are encouraged to take advantage of the access. You can observe many Master Teachers after school, tutoring students and creating after-school clubs for chess, investment practice, computer skills, rap, rites of passage, newspaper reading, martial arts, and whatever other activities the students are interested in. This is just one of the many reasons why Master Teachers are visited years later by their students with whom they have developed bonding and synergy. I was not surprised about the kindergarten teacher who became the common denominator for so many successful adults. Master Teachers make the difference.

When I was a classroom teacher, bonding was my primary objective during the first week. I'd ask students what career they wanted when they grew up. You're not at risk because you're low income and fatherless. You're at risk when you don't have goals. When the children stated their goals, I placed their career next to their name in my class roster. I then called on those students by their career for the entire school year. Can you imagine what it is like for a child to be called Dr. Darryl, Engineer Cathy, Esquire Denise, or Minister Kevin? The children began to believe in the possibilities. I'd also call them Mr. or Ms. to convey respect, and they returned it to me. I also encouraged them to refer to each other by their career or surname, which generated more respect among them. Consequently, there were few disciplinary problems in my classes.

Have you ever observed an Instructor's classroom? The walls are so drab, live children die in those classrooms. I believe that decor is essential, particularly for right-brained thinkers. It is extremely important for right-brained thinkers to learn in a stimulating environment. Unfortunately, from the fourth grade on the quality of classroom decor declines. I mentioned earlier that I don't believe decorating a classroom or a school with pictures of White male presidents is advantageous for African American students. In my classroom I had pictures of my students on the walls because they were my stars. I also had pictures of famous African American men and women.

Note the word h*is-story*. Most history books are male dominated. I wanted a balance of heroes and heroines. I also wanted a balance of historical and contemporary figures. One of my books *Great Negroes Past and Present Volume 2* provides a collection of contemporary famous African Americans. I wrote this in response to the many students who asked me, "Do you have to die to be famous?" I wonder where they got that notion?

Have you ever observed the chalkboard of a Master Teacher? You will not see anything on the chalkboard that is not related to the subject that is being taught at that moment. In contrast, information on the chalkboard of a Custodian, Referral Agent, or Instructor might be two days old. I recall visiting a classroom where, as early as 9:13a.m., the teacher had several boys' names on the board for negative behavior. My first question was, "How can they have their name removed?" She said, "Once you're on the board, you can't come off." You can imagine how the boys acted since they were aware that the punishment was for the entire day. I then asked, "Is there a positive section of the board?" She said, "No, only negative." I encouraged her to read the work of B.F. Skinner on behavior modification. The behavior you desire should be that which is reinforced. I pray the teacher did not subconsciously desire negative behavior. Children need attention, even if it is negative.

It is unfortunate, that only 5 percent of seniors feel good about their educational experience. It is tragic that there's an inverse relationship between age and questions asked. Unfortunately, there's a direct relationship between age and cheating. Many times schools invite me to speak to their students because they say the students lack motivation. But was there a lack of motivation in kindergarten? The longer students are with us, the less motivation they possess and the fewer questions they ask.

Custodians, Referral Agents, and Instructors ask more questions in class than students. The present ratio is 27:1. Fortunately, Master Teachers encourage students to ask the majority of the questions. It is a beautiful experience to observe a Master Teacher. I've been in some classrooms where the Master Teacher sat in a student chair and had a student teach the class. I've observed Master Teachers ask open-ended questions, knowing that they were endless answer possibilities. It has been a real treasure to observe students who listen to a Master Teacher admit that they do not know the answer to the question. It takes a great degree of security to admit to a student that you don't know the answer.

Master teachers are lifetime learners and they convey the message to children that learning never stops. If you want to "train" a child, you only ask what you already know. The scenario is that the student will know what the teacher knows. That is unacceptable for Master Teachers. Coaches believe that at some point students should exceed them, and that can only happen by encouraging students to ask the majority of the questions and for their own questions to be open-ended.

There was an excellent article written almost a decade ago that is just as relevant today. In "The Pedagogy of Poverty vs. Good Teaching," [13] Martin Haberman says, "Teaching acts that constitute the core function of urban teaching are giving information, asking questions, giving directions, making assignments, monitoring seat work, reviewing assignments, giving tests, reviewing tests, assigning homework, reviewing homework, settling disputes, punishing non-compliance, marking papers and giving grades."

The typical assignment outlined in "The Pedagogy of Poverty" is, take out your dictionaries and write the words that begin with H. This philosophy appeals to several constituencies:

1. It appeals to those who themselves did not do well in schools. People who have been brutalized are usually not rich sources of compassion, and those who have failed or done poorly in school do not typically take personal responsibility for that failure. They generally find it easier to believe that they would have succeeded if only somebody would have forced them to learn.

2. It appeals to those who rely on common sense rather than thoughtful analysis. It is easy to criticize human and developmental teaching aimed at educating a free people as mere permissiveness, and it is well known that permissiveness is the root cause of our nation's educational problem.

3. It appeals to those who fear minorities and the poor. Bigots typically become obsessed with need for control.

4. It appeals to those who have low expectations for minorities and the poor. People with limited vision frequently see value in limiting unfamiliar forms of pedagogy. They believe that at-risk students are served best by directive, controlling pedagogy.

Unfortunately, "The Pedagogy of Poverty" does not work. Youngsters achieve neither minimal levels of skill nor learn what they are capable of learning. The classroom atmosphere created by constant teacher direction and student compliance seethes with passive resentment that sometimes bubbles up into overt resistance. Teachers burn out because of the emotional and physical energy they must expend to maintain their authority every hour of every day. Teachers who began their careers as helpers, models, guides, stimulators, and caring sources of encouragement end up as directive authoritarians in order for them to function in urban schools.

The National Commission on Teaching recommends the following:

1. All children must be taught by teachers who have the knowledge, skills, and commitment to teach children well.

2. All teachers-education programs must meet professional standards or they will be closed.

3. All teachers must have access to high-quality professional development and regular time for collegial work and planning.

4. Both teachers and principals must be hired and retrained based on their ability to meet professional standards or practice.

5. Teacher salaries must be based on knowledge and skills.

6. Quality teaching must be the central investment of schools. Most education dollars will be spent on classroom teaching.

We can ill afford to lose Master Teachers to administration or corporate America. Uniform pay protects the worst at the expense of the best. Should custodians be paid the same as Master Teachers? We have very narrow standards for students. They include No Pass-No Play and denial of promotion unable to be promoted to the next grade or graduation if grades and test scores are unacceptable. Why the double standards? Teachers have unions and students do not.

Interestingly, 50 percent of private schools in the United States and many European countries operate on merit pay. Fortunately, many cities have chosen to do likewise. I believe if merit pay validated by peer, parent, and administrative review along with test scores and overall school performance, were instituted, we could successfully address the critics. While an entire book could be written on this subject, it's important to mention here because we are losing Master Teachers while Custodians, Referral Agents, and Instructors continue to increase numerically and prosper financially.

Finally, Master Teachers succeed because they work hard to bond with parents. To paraphrase the old adage, in order to be successful you need to walk in the shoes of your students. You need to walk through their neighborhoods. You need to observe their surroundings. Many Master Teachers visit the children's homes. They have created monthly potluck suppers and everyone brings a dish. There are academic contests, where the children perform in front of their parents. Master Teachers either recognize each child's birthday during the school day or group all the students born in a particular month to be acknowledged at the potluck supper.

While some schools complain about poor parent involvement, Master Teachers often have 100 percent parent attendance at after-school events–better than PTA meetings. Some Master Teachers even spend some time with students over the weekend or at church, the museum, zoo, ballgame, mall, piano recitals, etc., and may even provide this enrichment as a treat for their students.

In *Chicken Soup for the Teacher's Soul* Helen Mrosla told an excellent anecdote. The teacher had all students write the names of all their classmates pinpointing one positive attribute for each. The teacher then collated all the attributes awarded each child and gave each student his/her list. Unfortunately, one of the students died within a decade. At the funeral, the parents shared with the teacher his most prized possession. It was the sheet of paper with all of his attributes identified by his classmates. He kept it in his wallet for all his young life.[14]

In the following chapter, we will look at one of the major aspects of schools: the curriculum. How can we make curricula relevant for African American children?

Chapter Five

A Relevant Black Curriculum

- ❖ Culture is more than food, festivals, and music; it is way of life.
- ❖ True education transmits skill, a commitment to your race, a love for learning, and adoration for God.
- ❖ What is the impact on the Black student psyche to observe pictures of U.S. presidents in the school hallway?
- ❖ What the pupil wants to learn is as important, if not more so, than what the teacher wants to teach.
- ❖ A failing grade may indicate the degree of disconnection between student and curriculum, rather than student skills.
- ❖ Facts that are understood last longer than those memorized.

Why are so many African American children bored? Large numbers give up expecting school to make sense in their lives. Unfortunately, not only are African American children bored but most children are bored with school. This is tragic because they did not enter school bored. Ironically, the longer children are in school the more bored they become. They don't seem to be bored when they are outside of school. One of the most important questions any student could ask is, "Why do I have to learn this?" Tragically, many teachers view this as an act of defiance and belligerence. I believe students need to take an active role in their education. I don't believe that education belongs to teachers. The only way students are going to take an active role in their education is for them to be encouraged to ask, "Why do I have to learn this?" If teachers cannot answer the question, they should seriously consider whether or not they should teach the concept.

I also believe that education should create an endless desire to learn. I don't believe learning ceases with graduate degrees.

What must we do to make the curriculum relevant for African American children? What must we do to give them a burning desire to learn? Why do African American children need to know that Hippocrates was the first doctor and that Columbus discovered America? What is the significance of African American children being taught that Abraham Lincoln freed the slaves? What if I told you that the above three statements were false? Why do we lie to African American children? The Hippocratic Oath, acknowledges that the first doctor was an African named Imhotep. His Greek name was Aesculapius. I know it is hard for racists to accept that Africans discovered medicine before the Greek era. If a language arts teacher explains that to discover is to be first, is it possible for that same teacher to tell students that Columbus was first in America? During the Civil War, the South seceded from the Union. Abraham Lincoln did not have jurisdiction over the South. In the North, where he had jurisdiction, he did not free the slaves. The Emancipation Proclamation referred to slaves in the South, where he had no jurisdiction. The Thirteenth Amendment freed the slaves. Abraham Lincoln saved the Union and seriously reflected on what would be best for the country: to send African Americans back to Africa or to keep them in America? Capitalists in the North convinced Lincoln it would be better to keep Africans in America to work in their factories than to ship them back to Africa.

Unfortunately, Custodians, Referral Agents, and Instructors believe education is confined to the textbook. If it is not in the book, it cannot be taught. Consequently, students are receiving inaccurate information about Hippocrates, Columbus, Lincoln, and many others because the textbooks are wrong. Even

A Relevant Black Curriculum

if the information were true, the question remains, why do African American children need to learn this? why does an African American child living in the inner city need to know that Hippocrates was the first doctor? Or that Columbus discovered America? For the African American child living in the suburbs how can they apply to their own experience the knowledge that Abraham Lincoln freed the slaves? Why are we attempting to make African American children learn things that are irrelevant?

A Master Teacher has a desire, like other teachers, to help children master skills in language arts, mathematics, science, and social studies. A major difference between a Master Teacher and a Custodian is that Custodians confine themselves to the textbook. Master Teachers believe they can teach skills regardless of the content of the book. They realize that the student's environment is rich with content. Master Teachers use rap lyrics, cultural videos, TV shows, hip hop magazines, neighborhood billboards, local and national newspapers, and magazines—whatever does the best job.

Let me give you an overview of a relevant Black curriculum. We have developed a curriculum called SETCLAE (Self-Esteem Through Culture Leads to Academic Excellence). What do your African American students talk about with each other? What they talk about should be the focal point of your curriculum. What are the top five rap CDs? What are the top five Black television shows? Those shows are not the same for White America. What are the popular Black youth magazines? What are the problems in the community? The discussion and answers to these questions make up the foundation of the SETCLAE curriculum.

Every teacher of African American youth needs to know the top five rap CDs in Black America. If I want to teach language arts, can't I use some words from the rap CD? There would be a greater interest in language arts if we used the lyrics from the five most popular rap artists. It always amazes me how teachers say that African American youth can't learn, yet those same children can memorize a rap CD in three to five minutes, verbatim. If they can memorize a rap CD, could they not memorize the constitution, 50 names of states, and algebraic equations? We'll discuss that in the next chapter on African American Students.

I recommend that the teacher play a rap CD and ask the students to write all the words. Please note that stores sell the G and PG-rated versions of most CDs. Don't allow profanity in your classroom. The oral skills of African American youth exceed their written skills; however, they must learn to spell everything they say. Writing the words of the rap tune will be very enjoyable for the youth because that's all they talk about before and after school. They're now excited because there is synergy between their neighborhood life and school. After the children write all the lyrics, the Master Teacher will select words that will be used for this week's spelling test. We as educators simply want to teach our children how to spell. Why not use words that are part of the children's culture?

Rap lyrics can be used as both positive and negative examples to teach children capitalization, noun-verb agreement, sentence structure, grammar, and punctuation. African American children are fascinated by rap artists. If our desire is to increase reading skills, why don't we have them read about rappers? When was the last time you observed someone reading a book in which they had little interest? Unfortunately, that's what schools require. We expect students to read books that are uninteresting. If our children are fascinated by Puff Daddy, Snoop, Little Kim, MC

A Relevant Black Curriculum

Lite, and JayZ, let them read about them. If we want to teach poetry and rhyming skills, why not allow the youth to use rap as a catalyst into poetry and rhyme? In addition, all children need to write daily in their journals.

In the area of mathematics, why would we expect children to be motivated to learn multiplication, division, percentages, decimals, algebra, geometry, trigonometry, and calculus if they are simply told to go to a page and answer the first ten problems. In many schools, even when a word problem is provided, the context is outside the Black community. We must make the curriculum relevant and must give students the encouragement to learn.

Isn't it amazing how schools have "kicked out" students? Notice that I did not say they dropped out. They were "pushed out," and some of those same students, without pencil, paper, or calculator, can convert kilos to grams and grams to dollar bills! It is a sad commentary when gangsters can teach African American children math better than educators. When you ask many African American males what type of career they would like to have, invariably the first answer is not just athletics but specifically a career in the NBA. If our desire is to teach mathematics, then use the NBA to teach it. A Master Teacher could teach the four major mathematical operations addition, subtraction, multiplication, and division using the NBA. For example, questions could include the following:

How many teams are in the NBA?
How many players are on a team?
What is the total number of players in the NBA?
How many teams make the playoffs?

How many teams are eliminated?

How many players desire to make the NBA?

How many players are unsuccessful?

If a player signs a contract for $10 million and his agent receives 1 percent, how much does the agent receive?

If taxes are 38 percent, what does the government receive?

How many minutes are in a quarter of play? How many quarters are in a game?

What is the total number of minutes in a game?

If a player takes 21 shots and makes 14 what is his shooting percentage?

Teachers can use all sports in this way. With the advent of Title IX legislation, using sports to teach math will be relevant to both males and females. We could also use rap contracts to learn mathematics.

Let's move to the area of science. Before we go to Mars, Jupiter, and Venus, it may be more relevant to understand one's own body, melanin, lead poisoning, asthma, toxic waste sites, sickle cell anemia, AIDS, STDs, the relationship between cocaine and crack, and Type II diabetes. Lead poisoning is running rampant in the African American community. Almost 25 percent of African American children suffer from asthma. AIDS has now become the number-one killer of African American males and is number two for African American females. For some strange reason, the Justice Department gives a mandatory five-year sentence for the possession of 5 grams of the derivative crack cocaine and does not give any punishment for possessing 499 grams of the original source, cocaine. The following graph is an illustration of what drugs do to the brain.

A Relevant Black Curriculum

Let's now look at the social studies curriculum. Before we focus on Rome and Greece, if our desire is to teach history we could start with the history of our students. A nine-year-old child has a history. Ferreting it out will personally connect a child to the subject of history. Another good exercise is developing a family tree. Introduce students to Alex Haley and *Roots,* and challenge them to see how far back they can go in their family history. Use each receding generation to discuss historical events that took place within their family tree. In the 1990s, when they may have been born, talk about the Rodney King Rebellion. The 1980s could reference the Gulf War. In the 1960s and '70s exciting topics would include Martin Luther King, Malcolm X, and the Vietnam War. The 1950s was about Jim Crow and Brown vs. Topeka. Between 1900-1940, children could learn how their grandparents were affected by the Depression, the Northern Migration, Booker T. Washington, and W.E.B. Dubois.

87

The most exciting part of the social studies curriculum is the question, "What are the problems in the African American community?" If you ask students, they would probably mention gangs, drugs, unemployment, crime, and lack of jobs and recreation centers. As a Master Teacher, you would then show them how they can use their skills to address those problems. For example, if our children believe that drugs are a major problem, students could write letters to the Police Department, identifying the locations (which they already know) of alley stores and crack houses. They could also write to judges and to the mayor. Let them write letters to gang leaders to convince them of the importance of developing a truce. They could write sympathy letters to surviving family members of homicides. They could write letters to Nike and Michael Jordan, asking them why they use child labor and pay 17 cents a day to workers while charging $200 for shoes. The list is endless. The students are now learning concepts interesting to them, and educators are developing children's skills in language arts, mathematics, science, social studies, and civic responsibility.

Let me close this chapter with the classic story of Cinderella told from two different perspectives.

White version:

Once upon a time, there was a girl named Cinderella. She was very happy and she lived with her father. Her father remarried a woman who had three daughters. When Cinderella's father died, her stepmother treated Cinderella very badly and in fact made her the maid for herself and her three daughters. At the same time, in this land, the King decided it was time for the Prince

A Relevant Black Curriculum

to marry, so he sent a summons to all the people in the kingdom to come to a Ball. Cinderella was not allowed to go but was forced to help her stepsisters and her stepmother to prepare for the Ball. After they left for the Ball and as Cinderella was crying on the hearth, her Fairy Godmother came and with her magic wand gave Cinderella a beautiful dress, glass slippers, and a stagecoach made from pumpkins and mice. She then sent Cinderella to the Ball in style. There was one stipulation: she had to be back home by midnight. At the Ball, the Prince was completely taken with Cinderella and danced with her all evening. As the clock began striking midnight, Cinderella remembered what her Fairy Godmother had said and fled from the dance. All she left was one of her glass slippers. The Prince held a big search, using the glass slipper as a way to identify the missing woman. When he finally found Cinderella, she was identified because her foot fit the glass slipper. He married her and they lived happily ever after.

Africentric perspective:

Well you know Cinderella married the prince in spite of that old nasty stepmother. Pointy eyes that one old hag. Good thing she had a Fairy Godmother or she never would have made it to the Ball. Lucky thing, God bless her ragged tail. Wish I had me a Fairy Godmother and to think she nearly messed up big time by staying till the clock was striking twelve. After all the Fairy Godmother had done for her, hum, she should have known better. Eyes too full of the Prince, they were. They didn't call him the Prince for no reason. When she got to the Ball her stepsisters and stepmother didn't even recognize her, she was so beautiful without those rags, served them right, no-good jealous hags. The Prince just couldn't quit dancing with her, just couldn't take his eyes off of her, he had finally found his woman, lucky her, lucky him. Sure wished life was a fairy tale. Kind'a like the way I met Charlie, ha ha. The way she arrived was something else. A coach and a horseman, really fancy. Too bad that when she ran out of there as the clock struck twelve all that was left was a pumpkin rolling away and four mice. What a surprise for the mice. Well the Prince has to find her because his heart is broken. So he takes the glass slipper and hunts for her and her old wicked stepmother is hiding her. What a prize aren't they all? But he finally finds her and marries her. Somebody as good as Cinderella deserved that. Sure hope she never invites that stepmother to her castle, should make her the maid. [15]

Lisa Delpit describes how students respond differently to various versions of stories. Young White children have a tendency to tell topic-centered narratives, stories focused on one event. Black youngsters, especially girls, like to tell episodic narratives, stories that include shifting scenes and are typically longer. While these differences are interesting in themselves, what is of greatest significance is the adult responses to stories' differences.

A White adult was taped reading a story about Black and White first graders, with all syntax removed. Adults were asked to listen to the story, too, and comment about the children's likelihood of success in school. The researchers were surprised by the different responses given by Black and White adults. In responding to the reading of a Black child's story, the White adults were uniformly negative, making such comments as terrible story, incoherent, and not a story at all. Asked to judge this child's academic competence, all the White adults rated her below the children who told topic-centered stories. Most of these adults also predicted difficulties in this child's future school career. The child might have trouble reading, they thought, and she exhibited language problems that could hamper school achievement. The Black adults had very different reactions. They found the child's story well formed, easy to understand, interesting, and with lots of details.[16]

What Every African American Student Should Know
Who am I?
Where did my people originate?
When did the history of my people begin?
What are the differences between Negro and African history?
What have my people contributed?
Who was Imhotep? When were the Pyramids built and by whom?
What is the culture of my people?
Who oppressed my people?
Why are some people racists?
What did slaveholders do?
What took place in the 246 slave revolts?
How many Africans died due to slavery?

Who were King Ramses II, Queen Hatshepsut and Nzingha, Paul Cuffe, Martin Delaney, Frederick Douglass, Booker T. Washington, W.E. B. Dubois, Marcus Garvey, Martin Luther King, Malcolm X, Harriet Tubman, Phyliss Wheatley, Sojourner Truth, Fannie Lou Hamer, Mary McCloud Bethune, and Rosa Parks?
What is the present condition of my people?
What can I do to enhance the condition of my people?

The ball is now in the teacher's court. Are you going to teach what you want to teach and run the risk that your students will be bored and unreceptive? Or are you going to use the children's lifestyle as the cornerstone for teaching skills? Will you teach by the book or will you teach by the children? Are you going to teach the way you want to teach or the way children learn?

Chapter Six

African American Students

❖ Low-income children lack money, not intelligence.

❖ Why do many teachers give left-brain lesson plans to right-brain-thinking students?

❖ Are we expecting Black male students to act like White females?

❖ If you don't respect the children's culture, you negate their essence.

❖ The computer doesn't know I'm Black. It doesn't embarrass me in front of the class. It gives me another chance to solve the problem and helps me to succeed.

❖ To achieve academic success, students must select their friends wisely.

❖ Being in poverty is rarely about a lack of intelligence, but rather a lack of mentors, goals, and opportunities.

❖ Schools are virtually the only places where low-income students can learn middle-class values.

❖ Is it possible that some African American youth have not met any adult worthy of their respect?

❖ High school graduates who possess basic skills but are unable to think and are incapable of making moral choices become dangerous.

❖ Before we make workers, we must develop critical thinkers.

The Black family is not monolithic. Twenty-five percent of African American families earn in excess of $50,000 a year, while one-third of African American families live below the poverty line. I elaborated the fact that 50 percent of African American children also live below the poverty line. When you think of an African American student, who comes to your mind? Middle-income, lower-income, rural, city, or suburban students? Do they come from a two-parent home or single-parent home? The child could be male or female, light skinned or dark skinned, short or tall, neatly or poorly dressed. They could be in kindergarten or twelfth grade, honors, gifted and talented, advanced placement, remedial reading, or special education. There is a wide array of African American students.

Teachers shouldn't lower their expectations because students are Black, low income, fatherless, and poorly dressed. These are some of the traditional reasons why teachers lower expectations for African American students. Unfortunately, the African American students that receive the greatest brunt of disrespect and low expectations are inner-city African American males in the upper grades-dark skinned, speaking Ebonics, and trapped in remedial classes.

Many teachers believe that African American children, including boys, are cute in kindergarten, but that perception changes with each passing grade. Interestingly, I've had to tell teachers that the angriest boy in their class simply needs a smile. He may be tall, overweight, and look threatening, but all he needs is a touch, a smile, and a word of encouragement. Unfortunately, many teachers are not aware that one of the major reasons why many students are angry is because of fear. But you can't teach a child by exacerbating fear. The Bible reminds us that the perfect way to cast out fear is with love.

Sadly, many educators believe the racist research of Shockley, Jensen, and Murray. There is still a systemic position that African American children are genetically inferior. I would encourage all my readers to review *Developmental Psychology of the Black Child* by Amos Wilson. He compares the performance of African American and White infants. African American infants are able to hold their heads erect, recognize colors, and respond to stimuli much sooner than European children. Janice Hale's book *Learning While Black* is another must read. She compared the educational progress of children who had just entered Head Start with those who had been there for two years. She found that children who had just entered performed better, regardless of social demographics. The older children who attended Head Start the longest possessed lower scores. It is clear from Wilson and Hale that African American children enter Head Start ready to learn. Hale says, "African American children do not *enter* school disadvantaged, they *leave* disadvantaged. There's nothing wrong with the children but there is clearly something wrong with what happens to them in school."[17]

If Charles Murray, author of *The Bell Curve,* were sincere about wanting to compare the intelligence of children on the basis of race, the best time to start is not after they've been exposed to eight years of mis-education by an at-risk school but before they enter school. Instead, he describes the negative experiences that African American children have with an alien school system that is not compatible with their learning styles, a curriculum that is irrelevant, and teachers who fail to set high expectations or provide adequate time on task. What society labels an "achievement test" would be better described as an "exposure test." The many African American children who live below the poverty line and do not take summer trips to Europe, visit museums on weekends, or make the library a regular part of their educational experience suffer from this middle-class hegemony.

The million-dollar question is, what makes Black students unique? Ruby Payne would say poverty. If you want to understand African American youth, you must understand the hidden rules of poverty. Jeffrey Freed, the author of *Right Brained Children in a Left Brained World*, suggests that what makes African American children unique is that a large percentage of them are right-brained thinkers. Hale and many others would agree that a large percentage of African American students are right-brained thinkers. This is not to suggest that learning styles are dictated by genetics or income. There are low-income African American students living in the inner city who are left-brained (love math and science) and score over twelve hundred on the SAT. In contrast, there are right-brained White male children who live in affluent suburbs with both parents yet still are underachieving. Learning style is not dictated by race, income, or marital status. Culture is the driving force.

Payne says, "Some of the hidden rules in poverty are a high noise level, the television is always on, everyone may talk at once, the most important information is non-verbal, and the desire is to entertain."[18] What are the classroom implications if you have a large percentage of students coming from households where there are multiple stimuli occurring simultaneously? Left-brained thinkers perform better in a quiet environment with only one activity. In contrast, right-brained thinkers perform better with multiple stimuli and more noise.

Have you ever imagined a left-handed person using a right-handed toilet? In many schools, desks are designed for right-handed students. The door and the doorknob are built for right-handed people. Those examples illustrate how difficult it is for right-brained thinkers to excel in a left-brained school. Listed below are some additional differences between the two types of thinkers.

African American Students

Right-Brained People	Left- Brained People
Not good at remembering names.	Not good at remembering faces.
Respond best to instruction by example.	Respond best to written instruction.
Able to express feelings and emotions freely.	Not easily able to express feelings and emotions.
Prefer classes where they're studying or working on many things at once.	Prefer classes where there is only one assignment.
Good at thinking up funny things to say and or do.	Poor at thinking up funny things to say and or do.
Almost always can use whatever tools are available to get work done.	Prefer working with materials proper for the use they are intended for.
Respond emotionally. Skilled in showing movement and action.	Responsive to logical appeals. Skilled in written instruction.
Like to be in a noisy, crowded place where lots of things are happening at once.	Like to be where they can concentrate on one activity quietly.

Bernice McCarthy has developed the 4 Mat System. She believes there are four types of learners:

Innovative – Teachers need to create a reason for learning. Key question: Why?

Analytic – Teachers need to give them the facts. Key question: What?

Common Sense – Teachers need to let them try it. Key question: How?

Dynamic – Teachers need to let them teach themselves through discovery. Key question: If?

Unfortunately, most teachers' pedagogy is geared only for the Analytic learner. I encourage teachers to provide lesson plans for all four. Many African American students are Innovative and Common Sense learners.

What are the implications for teachers? How do we reconcile children who are excited about wanting to answer the question with teachers who want students to wait until recognized? Would you prefer 30 students acting like zombies or 30 eager beavers?

Let me describe call and response. In Black culture, there is no separation between the performer and audience. In White culture, there is such a separation. This is very similar to the classroom design, where there is separation between teacher and students. In Black culture, when the musician or speaker is performing, the audience is actively involved in the process. The audience may finish the sentence, say amen, or make comments to reinforce what is being said. They sing along with the musician. I have read stories where White participants were so hostile to African American involvement with the performer that they left the event.

Mainstream culture values visual learning through the written word. In the Euro-American tradition "seeing is believing," and it is commonly accepted that the highest levels of thinking are

African American Students

possible only for those humans who can reflect upon thoughts written down. Oral history and African griots are devalued. A geography teacher in the state of California discovered that her students, mostly Black and Latino males labeled remedial, scored considerably higher on a test when she read the questions provided. We can do this with all tests except state achievement tests. I would also suggest that since it has already been documented that achievement tests are culturally biased, measuring exposure more than achievement, and are not the best barometer for future performance, a minor concession would be to allow teachers to read the questions. Another teacher working with Black and Latino eighth graders in Texas found that their comprehension of a U.S. history text was better if they listened to a tape of the text while reading it. Her Anglo pupils preferred to read without hearing the tape.[19]

If only we had teachers that would be willing to make these minor adjustments. We could literally improve achievement scores on the Metropolitan, Iowa, California, and other achievement tests if the teachers simply read the questions to the students. If you know that many of your children prefer oral over visual, then why not change the pedagogy? It is amazing to me that psychologists, educators, and social workers espouse that African American children cannot learn and yet those same children can listen to a rapper's CD and in five minutes repeat the words verbatim. That is tremendous skill, and I've challenged teachers to try to do it themselves.

America is obsessed with the achievement tests. Testing on Monday and Friday is not advantageous for many African American students, especially those who live below the poverty line. For many African American students, their experiences over the weekend can preclude of the weekend could circumvent high test scores. Many educators suggest Wednesday as the best test day. This allows students time to calm down from the weekend and properly prepare for academics.

In my earlier books on education *Developing, Positive Self Images* and *Critical Issues,* I recommended learning centers. With all the research available, we still believe the only way to teach is with ditto sheets and textbooks. Try going all day Monday without ditto sheets and Friday without textbooks.

The five learning centers cover written material, oral material, pictures, fine arts, and artifacts. If we want to increase our success with African American children, we can no longer assume that all of them will learn from written materials. Children should be allowed to move from one learning center to another, and this hopefully will improve their understanding of the concept being taught. This approach mirrors the homes of children.

The following chart by Rosalie Cohen[20] gives us even more information to better understand the contrast between left-brained and right-brained thinkers, between the analytical style and relational style.

Left-Brained Students	Right-Brained Student
As it is in general	As it could be
(Analytical)	(Relational)
Rules	Freedom
Standardization	Variation
Conformity	Creativity
Memory of specific facts	Memory for essence
Regularity	Novelty

100

African American Students

Rigid order	Flexibility
"Normality"	Uniqueness
Differences equal deficits	Sameness equals oppression
Preconceive	Improvise
Precision	Approximate
Logical	Psychological
Atomistic	Global
Egocentric	Sociocentric
Convergent	Divergent
Controlled	Expressive
Meanings are universal	Meanings are contextual
Direct	Indirect
Cognitive	Affective
Linear	Patterned
Mechanical	Humanistic
Unison	Individual in group
Hierarchical	Democratic
Isolation	Integration
Deductive	Inductive
Scheduled	Targets of opportunity
Things focused	People focused
Constant	Evolving
Sign oriented	Meaning oriented
Duty	Loyalty

To be effective teaching African American students, you must convince them that there is a "payoff" in education. Experienced educators know that many African American youth believe they have a better chance of being successful by either becoming a professional ballplayer, securing a rap contract, or selling drugs. Effective teachers invite positive role models to speak to their students because often youth see athletes, rappers, and drug dealers but seldom have they talked to an engineer, computer programmer, or accountant. Unfortunately, what all of these have in common is an excessive desire for material wealth and consumption. One of the major reasons why African American adults buy cars, rent apartments, and have credit card debt that exceeds the rent payment is because of misplaced values and low self-esteem. Rap videos and their materialistic emphasis make our jobs as educators more challenging. I thought radio held our children captive, until I monitored the effect videos have on our youth. Watch the five most popular rap videos and then honestly assess how school curricula can compete for the minds of our youth.

My favorite question to African American youth is, "What are you going to be doing when you are 30 years of age?" More than half of all males answer professional sports and most choose basketball. To be effective with African American males, we must address this obsessive emphasis on sports. I encourage you to read *Hooked on Hoops* by Kevin McNutt. Most schools say very little about this issue, yet it is paramount for African American youth. One summer morning I watched 80 African American young men practice twice for their high-school football team. They would practice again in the afternoon. I'm an athlete and I value exercise, but I could not help wondering where the English, math, and science coaches were during the summer? Even if we had those coaches, would 80 African American males attend even once a day?

The other culprit is dealing drugs. How can the African American prison population rise from 100,000 in 1980 to 1.4 million in 2002 and schools remain silent? We must allocate time to discuss the pitfalls of selling drugs. Our youth are more

African American Students

interested in crack than Columbus, liquor than Lincoln, and heroin than Hippocrates.

No significant learning takes place without a significant relationship. One of the reasons why African American youth achievement declines with each passing year is departmentalization. This allows students to be taught by different teachers for each subject. If you understand African American youth, you must understand their need for bonding and nurturance, regardless of age. The worst environment for an African American student is a large high school. Can you imagine an African American male right-brain thinker among 4,000 students being taught by five different Custodians throughout the day while his mind is on the latest rap CD, basketball playoffs, and selling crack cocaine? This feeds the dropout rate that hovers near 50 percent in some cities.

In Japan, students remain with their teacher for a minimum of two years. In Germany it could extend to four years. Both countries realize the importance of relationship. In addition, they both understand it is a terrible waste of time every September to learn new names, establish new rules, and review last year's work to assess where to begin in the new school year. For more than 30 years, studies of school organization have shown that the ideal size high school is 400 students. These schools often create interdisciplinary teams of teachers. Therefore, rather than a typical high school teacher having 5 classes of 30 students for 45 minutes each, at these "restructured" schools, a teacher has 20 students for 90 minutes. They have less students and classes, but they have students longer and either team teach or teach two subjects. The National Center for Restructuring Education, Schools, and Teaching (NCREST) has championed this movement for over a decade. We could reduce the dropout rate if we improved the student-counselor ratio. In many inner-city high schools the ratio is 500:1. How much counseling can occur with that ratio? Why do African American youth have to become incarcerated before receiving individual attention?

It is difficult for African American teenagers to move from one teacher to another teacher every 45 minutes if the bond has not been established. It is even more difficult for African American students to adjust to a first period Custodian, a second period Referral Agent, a third period Instructor, a fourth period Teacher, and a fifth period Coach. Of course, if departmentaliza-tion were abolished, we'd run the risk of having a Custodian in charge the entire school day. Still, departmentalization needs to be reevaluated.

Earlier, I mentioned that many African American students divide teachers into two categories: Those who fear them and those who don't. Lisa Delpit describes a communication problem between teachers and many African American students. The teacher often sends children to the office for disobeying their directive. In middle-class White culture, adults often "suggest" to children what they want them to do. For example, "Don't you think it's time for you to start reading?" The adult is actually telling the child what to do. But in Black culture, in most cases transcending income, the child thinks he is being given an option and can choose to read. The child does not believe he is being defiant. Parents are frequently called in for conferences. The parent's response to the teacher is usually the same: "They do what I say. If you just tell them what to do, they'll do it." Black children expect an authority figure to act with authority.

When a teacher instead acts as a "chum," the message sent is that this adult has no authority and children act accordingly.

African American Students

In other words, the authoritative person gets to be a teacher because she is authoritative.[21] Some members of middle-class culture, by contrast, expect the teacher to be the authority because she is the teacher. The authoritative role ordains authoritative status.

Ruby Payne does not believe this will work with many African American students. She says that many African American students laugh when they are disciplined.[22] This can truly irritate a teacher, but it is simply another self-defense mechanism by African American students as they respond to the conflict of culture and values.

I believe the most important subject is reading. Over 90 percent of African American inmates enter prison illiterate. Notice that I used the word entered because after they are incarcerated, they read more than most "free" people. Unfortunately, they had to become incarcerated in order to experience the joy of reading. One of the major lessons that I learned from author Jeffrey Freed is that as much as I am an advocate of phonics, it is more beneficial to left-brained thinkers who think in the abstract and are comfortable separating letters, words, and ideas from each other. Phonics is not the best approach to reading for a right-brained thinker who needs to see the whole picture first. This does not mean that phonics should be excluded from the curriculum for right-brained thinkers, but it should not be the learning foundation for someone who operates in the relational style.

In addition, right-brained thinkers are visual and create mind images when they read. They do not benefit from reading aloud. Unfortunately, many African American children have been embarrassed for their poor oral reading skills. This practice is seldom used in the workplace. There are a few positions, e.g., radio and television broadcasters, wherein it is valued, but reading aloud is not something done normally in our society. I wonder why teachers have children read aloud? It's not the best tool for cooperative learning, improving attention span, or increasing time on task. It is not the best tool for classroom management because once a child has finished reading, seldom do they listen to the other students waiting their turn. Right-brained thinkers create images in their minds while reading. Reading aloud slows the process. Surprisingly, right-brained thinkers are excellent speed readers.

Another critical subject is mathematics. The achievement gap is wider here than in reading. While other students are being exposed to algebra in middle schools, many African American students never take algebra because they drop out before being eligible. Algebra is the language of computers and the gatekeeping subject for college admission. It is a travesty that affluent White children receive algebra in fifth grade, and low-income, fatherless African American children receive it in eleventh grade.

Eleanor Orr in the excellent book *Twice as Less* documents that Black dialect can interfere with mathematical thinking. For example:

Standard English	Black dialect
Half of	two times less than
Half as large as	two times smaller than
	twice as less
	twice as small as

African American Students

Half as much as	half as small as
	half less than
Half as fast as	twice as slow as
	half as slow as

In reviewing the above, your answers will be very different if you calculate half of 20 rather than twice as less. How many teachers have been trained by education departments to cope with this phenomenon?

Negative peer pressure could have been a chapter by itself. It is very possible that parents and teachers could be effectively doing their job yet see it all go for naught because the Black peer group has not bought into academic achievement. Some would say that what makes African American students unique are their values. They tend to be cooperative. An historical African value is, "I am because we are." It is difficult for African American, Hispanic, or Native American students who value cooperation to excel in an environment that promotes competition and rugged individualism.

In one of my earlier books, *To Be Popular or Smart: The Black Peer Group*, I describe how African American students who are doing well in school are often teased by their peer group. Males are stripped of their masculinity and African American students are accused of acting White.

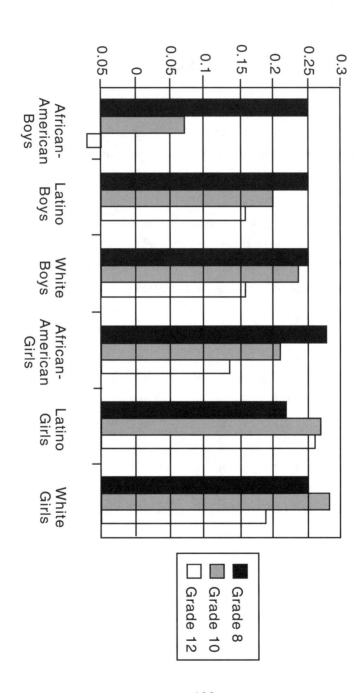

Trends in Identification with Academics

108

African American Students

One of the major reasons why Beverly Tatum wrote *Why are African American Children Sitting in the Cafeteria?* is because African American students feel school, especially an integrated school, is an alien place and that the only time they can relax among themselves is in the cafeteria. Ironically, when White students sit together in the cafeteria it is not questioned.

African Americans like Whites do not prefer being the minority in the class. This happens often for African American students in advanced placement, honors, gifted and talented, and at White colleges. When African American students feel they have to "represent" the race their test scores suffer. Their scores are much better without the racial pressure.

In order for us to effectively educate African American students, we must infiltrate the power of peer pressure. It is the number one influence on African American youth. Thus it is naive for educators to try to educate African American students if the Black peer group does not value academic achievement.

I would also encourage my readers to read the work of John Ogbu, who describes the impact of involuntary and voluntary minority groups. Involuntary minority groups become incorporated into a nation through conquest, slavery, or colonization. Voluntary minority groups become incorporated into a nation through voluntary emigration. Involuntary groups tend to oppose the cultural values of the majority to prevent conquerors, slavers, and colonizers from wiping out their indigenous culture. They feel that they cannot adopt any of the ways of the majority without giving up parts of their culture. Voluntary minorities differ from involuntary minorities in that they generally tolerate the new culture or even wish to be assimilated into it.

African Americans (through slavery), Native Americans (through conquest), Puerto Ricans (through colonization), Mexican Americans (through conquest of the Southwest) are classified as involuntary minorities. Involuntary minorities see school as a majority institution, which means that the academic achievement it promotes challenges their group loyalties and ethnic identities. Voluntary minorities are secure in their ethnic identities, but they want to learn new ways that will enable them to succeed in their new country. For them, this will lead to new opportunities. Asian Americans constitute voluntary minorities. They use schooling as a path to achievement in a broader society. Unlike the experiences of involuntary minorities, the dominant culture has never actively eradicated the culture and language of voluntary immigrants.

The media loves comparing immigrants to slaves. The favorite comparison is Asian to African. Asian students are viewed as the ideal and African American as the most challenging. There are far more Asians than African Americans in gifted and talented classes. Do schools expect African American students to act like Asian students? What can African American students learn from Asians? First, Asians believe in time on task. Their number of study hours exceeds all groups. Second, they use peer pressure positively, by studying together. Third, their parents believe they themselves are the primary educators. Last, their culture inspires them to excel similar to our Rule 110 before we lost it with integration.

I would also encourage you to read Murrell's *African-Centered Pedagogy*. While he appreciates Ogbu's argument, he believes it does not fully explain why so many African American children associate being smart with acting White. The Black mind set is not shaped solely by our "arrival status" but also includes

African American Students

staff demographics, expectations, pedagogy, curriculum, role models, family, media, and community viability.

How do we change the mind set that being smart is acting White? It's difficult for this ideology to change if African Americans students are in schools with very few African American teachers. Role modeling is significant, and it is very difficult for African Americans to strive to be engineers, doctors, computer programmers, and accountants when they are exposed to so few Blacks in those professions. In contrast, they are exposed to many Black athletes and entertainers. Teachers should invite, on a weekly basis, positive role model African Americans, preferably male, to speak about math and science and the professions.

It's going to be difficult to change this mind set if African American history is confined to the shortest month of the year and taught incorrectly. It is understandable why so many African American youth associate being smart with being White when their history begins in slavery and is taught in only 28 days. It would be constructive if African American youth were taught their history throughout the year, beginning with building pyramids rather than being enslaved on plantations. Unfortunately, most teachers, including African Americans, know more about Black history after 1619 than before 1619.

I have never met an African American child who knew that Imhotep was the father of medicine associate being smart with acting White. I have met numerous African American students who thought that Hippocrates was the first doctor and associated being smart with acting White. I believe people who have a solid understanding of their history do not make asinine statements, such as being smart is acting White.

Ruby Payne analyzes cooperative values from a poverty perspective. Take the case of a lady in church who receives some extra money and is immediately besieged with requests. One of the hidden rules of poverty is that any extra money is shared. Middle-class values place great emphasis on being self-sufficient. Lower-class values teach that one never gets ahead and when extra money is available, it is shared or immediately spent. There are always emergencies and needs, so one must enjoy the moment. The lady will share the money. She has no choice. If she does not, the next time she is in need, she will be left in the cold. It is a hidden poverty rule that people can only rely on each other. This reinforces the famous religious philosopher, John Mbiti and the African proverb, "I am because we are."

So what is it about middle-class culture and values that makes people believe, "I have mine and you have to get yours"? One student receives a 100 on a test and another receives 40. How many schools encourage the student with the higher grade to assist the other? From an African frame of reference, Black children enter the classroom with the desire to do things together. It is an alien school that attempts to teach African American children that they are islands unto themselves and that only the strongest survive. If we are going to effectively educate African American children, we need to change the value system. One of the best ways to resolve this issue is by using the buddy system. Teachers can divide the class into pairs so that buddies are responsible for each other. It is naive for us to expect African American children who do everything together at home, in the community, and on the playground to do things separately in the classroom.

Low-achieving and disadvantaged students are almost by definition unable to compete in regular school programs.

African American Students

Competition for them means coming in last and receiving failing grades. In cooperative learning programs, all students must perform well. It is the role of each student to assist the other. Also, in the act of assisting one another, learning is enhanced. Cooperation builds confidence and self-esteem, improves test scores by two stanines, while reducing disciplinary problems. An environment where all students are expected—and assisted—to do well is a place where a student can feel secure.

Cooperative learning is student centered. There is more time on task because it reduces disciplinary problems. I will never forget an experience with a low-achieving high school. I recommended cooperative learning. Weeks later, I observed former gang members outside on the school grounds drilling each other for their next-period biology class!

Children who fail in competitive, grade-oriented classrooms need cooperative learning to keep them from becoming casualties. Competition is only motivating for those students who have sufficient skill and ability to succeed. Grades are only motivating for those students able to glean good grades. In competitive classrooms, low-achieving students finish last, and it becomes demoralizing. In competitive environments, failing students cheat. There is less temptation to cheat with cooperative learning. Failing students have a greater propensity to create disciplinary problems. They use bad behavior as a smokescreen, hoping they will be removed from their failing classroom experience. In contrast, cooperative learning groups hold each other accountable academically and socially.

I once observed a teacher who allowed everyone in the class to simultaneously answer questions. The purpose of this "choral" response mode was twofold: to keep everyone alert and to build confidence. Children are able to give a wrong response yet have it blend in with correct answers. The "choral" response makes shy children feel more secure.

It is wise to identify and groom student leaders in the classroom. Many teachers think they are the leaders of the class, but they fail to realize that their students are taking cues from their peer leader. Once a student leader is sold on academic achievement, the rest of the class will come along.

In addition, I recommend the Jigsaw Method, the Team Assisted Approach, and the Nguzo Saba Assembly program. The Jigsaw Method requires the teacher divide the total number of students into equal-member teams. (No more that five members per team.) The assignment could be the life of Martin Luther King. Each member of the team would get a piece of the puzzle. One member would have information on King's childhood. Another member would have materials on his Morehouse experience. Another would have data on nonviolence and Mahatma Ghandi. The fourth member would have material on King's family, and the last member would have data on his career. The beauty of the Jigsaw Method is that each member of a team is dependent upon the other for information. As a result, you could have an A student in the group with a D student, but the A student is not going to be successful without the D student. The Jigsaw Method makes everyone dependent on one another. Everyone is important and each is as strong as the weakest link on the team.

In the Team Assisted Approach, teachers divide the students based on ability, so that every team would have an A, B, C, D, and F student. There would be equitable distribution of students in each group. One of the benefits of cooperative learning is that it discourages grading on a curve. In a typical classroom where teachers grade on the curve, the students with the highest grades are resented. Cooperative learning reverses that mind set, so honor roll students are desired because their scores improve the overall score of the team.

Unfortunately, schools give more accolades to athletic achievement than academic achievement, but in the Nguzo Saba Assembly program, all children can be recognized. Because schools operate from a middle-class, individualistic, competitive value system, awards are given to only a few. If African Americans participate in an academic assembly and witness very few students receiving awards, they will label those students nerds, sellouts, and acting White. The negative mind-set will continue. In the Nguzo Saba Assembly if a student moves from a D to a C, he/she receives an award. If a student moves from a C to an A, he/she receives two awards. Thus every student in the assembly could receive an award. With this program and others, it is very possible that African American students may buy into academic achievement.

Peer pressure does not have to be negative. In fact, we must create positive peer pressure by rewarding young scholars with memberships to the NAACP's ACT-SO program and the Urban League's Thurgood Marshall Achievers. Young people benefit from the experience of being with national scholars. They also enjoy flying around the country and staying in luxurious hotels.

Jeff Howard has developed the Efficacy Program to understand the psychology of success.[23] Unfortunately, many schools are integrated on the outside but highly segregated in their activities–the basketball team is all African American and the science club and debate team are all White. Jeff Howard's research has helped me better understand the psychology of why 200 African American students are willing to try out for 12 basketball slots, but are unwilling to try for slots on the debate team and science team where there is far less competition.

What explains this behavior? Howard says people who feel good about themselves attribute their success to their ability and effort alone. They attribute their failure solely to effort. In this way, they are always in control. If they fail, they know they simply have to increase time on task to improve. They understand the secret to success: "Whatever you do most will be what you do best." Unfortunately, students who have not grown proficient in the psychology of success attribute their success to luck or the nature of the task. They attribute their failure to ability. Therefore, if they do well on a math test, they attribute it to luck or the nature of the test. If they fail, they quickly question their ability and are no longer interested in studying. Unfortunately, African Americans have bought into this negative psychology and have convinced themselves that they are better in sports than science, music than math, and rap than reading.

If we are going to effectively educate African American students, everyone, teachers and students, must understand the psychology of performance. They need to understand the significance of ability, effort, luck, and the nature of the task. They need to realize that both success and failure should be attributed to their ability and effort. This way, they will always be in control. How many schools have taught African American students the psychology of performance?

In closing, the last area that I would like to analyze comes as a result of speaking at a social workers' conference. A social worker told me that the root of the problem in her school district was that they did not know how to channel Black male energy. I had written about this subject in several books, but I could not have said it clearer. *The root problem is that we do not know how to channel Black male energy.* It is mandatory that we learn how to do this. Otherwise, these students must pay the price by sitting in corners, principal's offices, remedial reading and special education classes, and by being suspended and expelled.

Why is it that in most elementary schools physical education is offered once a week but at the high-school level it is offered daily? If we are having problems channeling Black male energy, physical education should be a daily regimen in elementary schools. Ironically, we could reduce special education dollars by allocating more money to physical education. Second, I would suggest that every school offer non-combative martial arts. This will enhance self-discipline while releasing pent up energy.

In my earlier book, *State of Emergency: We Must Save African American Males*, I mentioned that some schools are now being built without playgrounds and recess has been removed from the school's schedule. Even though some schools have done this for security reasons and while I understand their concern, it is a critical mistake. Every school needs to offer recess and playground equipment. But the answer to channeling Black male energy is not limited to physical education and the need for recess and playground equipment. Upon the conclusion of every lesson, let children stretch, perform push-ups, or do something physical for five minutes before moving on to the next mental exercise.

In one of my earlier books, *Satan, I'm Taking Back My Health!*, I documented that Americans have increased their sugar consumption from 4 pounds to 155 pounds annually.[24] Our bodies were not designed to absorb that much sugar. As a result, diabetes and hyperactivity are pervasive. I strongly encourage principals to reduce if not eliminate sugar from their schools.

I encourage everyone to read Michael Guiran's book *Boys and Girls Learn Differently!* He documents from a scientific perspective that gender differences influence learning. For example, boys produce less serotonin and therefore are more impulsive. Males produce more testosterone, contributing to their aggression, in contrast to females who produce more estrogen, which has a more calming effect. Females have 20 percent more nerve tissue connecting right-and left-brain hemispheres. This explains their advanced verbal and reading skills. Boys have three times more reading difficulties than girls.

If we want to maximize the achievement of African American students, we need to give them more nurturing, fairness, appreciation of their culture, cognizance of sports, rap, and drugs, right-brain lesson plans, and cooperative learning. At the same time, administrations must focus on the psychology of performance, better utilization of Black male energy, and the elimination of departmentalization. When a student is retained, the burden should not just be borne by the student. The next year the retained student should receive the following:

* Master teacher * Africentric curriculum
Right brain lessons * longer school day
cooperative learning * smaller student : teacher ratio

In the next chapter, African American Parents, I will explore what parents can do to effectively complement teachers.

Chapter Seven

African American Parents

❖ Ineffective teachers blame parents.

I wish parents could hear what some teachers say about their children. Schools should make classrooms and teachers' lounges available to parents, not that teachers would make derogatory comments about their children in their presence, but I think that it would be a deterrent. I wonder how Mrs. Little, Malcolm X's mother, would have responded if she had heard the teacher tell Malcolm that he could not be a lawyer but was more suited to be a carpenter?

When I speak to parents, one of their frequent comments is that they cringe whenever they receive a call from the school. Unfortunately, most schools only interact with parents when there is bad news. Many teachers only give attention to students when they are "acting out." It should be no surprise that the way many educators teach students is the same way they interact with parents. How nice it would be if schools flipped the script and reported good news. How refreshing it would be for parents to receive a call from the school because their child received an A or B on their last reading or math quiz.

The major premise of this book is that there is a class and cultural conflict between African American students and middle-class schools, and I'd be remiss if I didn't address the issues that Black parents face.

Here's one example. During class, the teacher reviews math problems 1 through 10 and assigns problems 11 through 20 for homework. But there is one additional step in problems 11 through 20 that was not discussed during the school day. The school, in essence, expects the parents to become assistant teachers and tutor the children on materials not covered in school. This is acceptable if the parents have the educational background. For middle-class students this is the norm. Possibly middle-class teachers commit this error so often because they assume that the parents will be able to help the child. In Black and many other homes this is not always the case. As I mentioned earlier, this further explains why many African American children's scores decline after the fourth grade, as homework increases and there is no assistant teacher in the home. Also, in affluent homes parents can afford to hire tutors.

The Individual Educational Plan (IEP) meeting to determine the need for special education placement also causes problems for parents. If the meeting were parent-centered, it should be scheduled in the evening. Why should parents have to miss work? People with power have a difficult time imagining what it is like being a minority. This may explain the phenomenon described in the book *Why Are All The Black Children Sitting Together in the Cafeteria?* People gravitate to their comfort zone. It is also a trend in the housing industry: when neighborhoods exceed 10 percent African American, White flight ensues. I wonder how White students feel when they are in the minority in an African American classroom. This seldom happens because people with power seldom place themselves in those situations. The design of the IEP meeting offers no power to parents.

The IEP meeting is more intimidating if the four professionals are White. Many African American teachers have told me how challenging it is even for them to protect their biological children in an IEP meeting or a teacher-parent conference. You can imagine that if it is difficult for an African

African American Parents

American teacher who understands the system far better than a low-income African American parent, it must be very frightening for average parents.

In IEP meetings and teacher-parent conferences, many insensitive middle-class educators often use a vernacular that is not understood by parents. Educated people can communicate with anyone; but when you are trained in a certain profession's lingo, you might become arrogant, condescending, and talk down to the uninitiated. Why would an educator use a 16-letter word with a marginally educated parent? Some teachers in teacher-parent conferences remind parents that they have the degrees and therefore understand the child better than the parent. It takes a very secure parent to sit in an IEP meeting with highly educated individuals who are speaking above them and calmly provide alternative strategies and recommendations.

In my counseling to African American parents nationwide, I have recommended the following IEP strategies:

- Bring an advocate who understands the law and children's rights, such as a Black social worker, psychologist, educator, or community activist.

- Bring a copy of *Countering the Conspiracy to Destroy Black Boys, State of Emergency: We Must Save African American Males;* Michael Guiran's book *Boys and Girls Learn Differently;* and Mary Block's book *No More Ritalin.* Ask them if they knew that boys and girls have different learning styles and inquire as to what they have done to alter their lesson plans. Incidentally, African American females are also disproportionately placed in special education in relation to White females.

- Ask the principal if there is an equitable distribution of referrals among the staff.

- Ask if there are more males than females being referred and why.

- Ask the principal what he/she is doing to respond to any disparity.

- Was your child labeled last year? If not, what has changed?

- Ask that your child be transferred to the teacher with the least propensity to refer.

- Suggest creating a Black male classroom or a right-brained classroom.

- Suggest adding special education resources to the mainstream classroom.

- Provide a video tape of your son that documents his attention span either reading a book or playing games like checkers or Concentration.

- Suggest that your child go to a special education resource class for a maximum of one hour daily.

- Ask how special education classes are evaluated.

- Ask how soon children are mainstreamed (put back in a standard classroom) and if they return to the mainstream classroom at grade level.

African American Parents

I also recommend to parents that they reduce the sugar consumption in their child's diet. Reduce if not eliminate television, enroll their child in martial arts and rites of passage programs, and provide them with greater opportunities to learn about their interests on the Internet.

The other critical meeting is the teacher-parent conference. This meeting is to review the report card or progress report. This could also be another intimidating experience that promotes middle-class values. Many teachers stroke the ego of parents with the following comment: "Your child has the potential, but he/she is not applying himself/herself." The teacher knew that if she had told the parent that her child was slow and lacking intelligence there would be a major problem. What is amazing about this comment is that the adults, the teacher and the parent, look to the child to explain his/her poor performance. I am not against an individual taking responsibility for his/her behavior and performance, but the person with the primary responsibility is the one being paid. The burden of the child's grade should not be exclusively borne by the child. Parents should ask the following questions in the conference:

1. What were the child's reading and math scores at the beginning of the school year?
2. What are the teacher's goals for year end?
3. What are the teacher's strategies to achieve those goals?
4. What is the homework policy?
5. What is the grading policy?
6. What has been the teacher's track record over the years concerning statewide averages?
7. What can I do to assist you?
8. Each quarter, let's review progress on achieving the teacher's goals for the child.

This way, the responsibility is no longer exclusively borne by the child but by the teacher and parent. I encourage parents to join the Urban League's Standard Keepers program, which educates and empowers parents in their interaction with schools.

Schools say they want parents to be involved. I wonder. Involved to do what? Do schools really want to share power with parents? Do schools want parental input as part of the curriculum? Can you imagine the uproar if the PTA recommended an Africentric curriculum? If African American parents recommended more right-brained lesson plans and less reliance on ditto sheets and textbooks, how would that be received? Do schools really want to share power with parents or do they want parents to make baked goods and sell raffle tickets? Whether a school is public or private, parents own the school via their taxes or their tuition.

Unfortunately, many parents share with me their reasons for not attending PTA meetings: they simply do not feel welcome. I have suggested to principals that one of the first steps toward creating a more welcoming climate is to provide training for receptionists. I could describe horror stories of schools that were built 40 years ago, and the same secretary is still preventing parents from visiting classrooms and meeting with principals. Many students have told their parents that they would rather they not make waves for fear of repercussions. The school schedule is not designed for working parents. It is designed for the Leave It to Beaver family, where the father works and the mother stays home and is in a position to visit the school between nine and three o'clock.

One of the major differences between White and Black middle-class families that both earn $50,000 is that in White homes there is the possibility that it is all earned by the father. In Black homes it's usually two parents who earn $25,000 each.

African American Parents

Unfortunately, in 66 percent of African American homes the father is not present and mothers are working and have schedules that do not complement the school schedule.

I know that many educators reading this chapter will question my position because of the abysmal lack of parental involvement in the Black community. I concur that there are major problems. It is very frustrating for me to speak at a school and only 15 out of 300 parents attend. It would be very easy for me to chime in with the teachers' lounge discussion that Black parents do not care about their children. But my 30 years of experience have given me numerous success stories of schools that do enjoy significant parent involvement.

I had the fortunate privilege of speaking in a particular city on two consecutive nights. The first night's school had 22 parents in attendance. The second night's school, in the same district with the same demographics, had attendance that exceeded 200 parents. What explains the disparity? Should we continue to make negative comments about poor parent involvement? Should we continue to study failure or are we willing to study success? What did the second school do that the first school did not? Read James Comer's book *Waiting for A Miracle*. It reinforces a need for a village to embrace both school and home. I now send an advance parent marketing strategy to schools to increase attendance. The second school utilized the following strategies:

1. Let the parents choose the topic.

2. Chose an alternative site for the meeting rather than the school, preferably a progressive church or community organization venue.

3. Provide a full meal, not refreshments.

4. Have the children perform. The more children performing, especially in the lower grades, the more parents will be in attendance. Place them throughout the program and have them all perform at the end.

5. Offer a prize for the class that has the greatest number of parents in attendance.

6. Provide a door prize.

7. Provide child care and transportation.

8. Give parents responsibilities that help implement the program.

9. Offer a special prize for men that will entice them to attend.

10. Let the parents choose the day and time. They would not choose a day with popular television shows. Most would also not choose Wednesday due to Bible study. In addition, why are most elementary graduations during the work day? Why do 300 parents have to miss work rather than ask a few appropriate staff members to work late?

In the Black community there is a wealth of dynamic speakers. There could be an interesting topic and all of the above enticements could be in effect, but without a good speaker, parents' night will not be well attended. Provide the meal after the presentation. Unfortunately, I've attended events where the parents ate the food and left before the speaker began. I've also seen parents leave after their children performed. It is imperative that

African American Parents

children be placed throughout the program and that they all perform together after the speaker is finished. It is unfortunate that we have to create these marketing techniques, but because we have not shared power with parents, they feel unwelcomed and have not been encouraged to feel like the owners of the school. It is a contradiction to talk down to an illiterate parent and then expect them to be supportive.

Hopefully, these marketing strategies will only be necessary in the short term. From a long-term perspective, we need to empower parents. Study the success of Head Start. I think it is a tremendous illustration of empowerment when a low-income, illiterate parent can become a teacher assistant, teacher, and ultimately director of the program. Head Start reserves room for parents. They hire a Parent Coordinator to teach empowerment. Sadly, many parents who were empowered in the Head Start experience become powerless when their child enters the kindergarten through twelfth regime. This creates confusion for parents, who know when they are welcomed and when they are not.

We must also remember that parents are younger these days. It is possible that the parent is 13, the grandmother is 26, the great grandmother is 39, and the great great grandmother is 52. There are many teachers who have educated four generations of children in the same family. If we know that parents are younger in a certain school or district, then before we invite them to a workshop on their child's development, we may need to provide a workshop on developing their own self-esteem, male-female relationships, and more.

If we want more men present, we need to provide workshops on employment and entrepreneurship. Over the years, I have suggested to social workers that it is a middle-class feminine approach to expect men to sit around a conference table on a weekday morning drinking coffee, eating donuts, and discussing child care. If we want more men to be involved, the meeting should take place in a wood shop or electronics area. We could discuss child rearing while shooting free throws on the basketball court. How many social workers and educators think like that? Why do so many middle-class people think that meetings can only take place inside a conference or classroom?

Communication styles are another source of conflict. How do we reconcile the fact that the school says that when someone hits you tell a teacher, and the parents say that when someone hits you hit them back? Have schools ever thought about how African American children live after 3:00 P.M. how they survive on the streets where, unfortunately, adults are not present? Please don't misunderstand. I'm in favor of the school's position that children should not hit each other and should inform an adult when that happens. But I want schools to understand that students might have been taught differently at home and on the street. Schools need to discuss this with parents because children suffer when parents and teachers set rules that are inconsistent.

Also if we want children to tell an adult, we need staff who will dispense discipline fairly. Russell Skiba from the University of Indiana documented the fact that school punishment was distributed unfairly. There was a disproportionate percentage of African American males suspended and expelled. He cited numerous incidents where Black and White children have committed the same infraction.[25] The White child was asked to write a paper while the African American child was suspended for three days.

If schools want African American children to inform them, they must be fair and consistent. They also need to provide adults not just in the classroom but in the cafeteria, on the playgrounds, and within a reasonable radius between school and home. Schools must also work with parents, community activists, ministers, and recreational leaders to create a village for youth. One of the major reasons why so many African American children join gangs is because they have not received protection from adults.

When teachers request parents to attend a meeting because of their child's behavior, the problem is that the parent will be the only one in attendance who lacks information. This being the case, some parents have automatically taken their child's side and have even cursed the teacher in front of their child.

In my book *Restoring the Village: Solutions for the Black Family* I discuss the village in detail. Historically, parents and teachers were on the same side. What happened to the trust? How can it be restored? One of the major reasons why parents believe their child's story and not the teacher's is because they take the negative behavior of their children personally and feel it's a reflection on them. They are in denial and refuse to listen to anyone disciplining their child. How naive to believe that only one person can raise your child in this new millennium, with all the negative obstacles facing us.

Some parent's communication style is emotional and loud. In middle-class culture, people communicate calmly and softly. I remember when I debated in college we were taught to see issues objectively and not emotionally. It was not about personal right or wrong; it was an abstract discussion. Maybe that can explain how lawyers can dispassionately represent guilty clients.

Schools often tell me that African Americans are too emotional and bring too much passion to the issue. Ruby Payne says that when a discussion is taking place about bad behavior, those parents who agree with the teacher will chastise the child and promise the teacher that it will not happen again. The teacher believes the parent. Unfortunately, African American parents view discipline differently. Yes, they chastise the child and promise the teacher that it won't happen again, but that same parent will make sweet potato pie for their child later that evening.[26]

In many African American homes there is much inconsistency. I have observed hundreds of parents who will slap the child one moment and hug the child the next. They will tell the child that he or she will never amount to anything one moment and the very next moment compliment the child and make their favorite dish. In lower-income homes, food is used as a treat or pacifier. Unfortunately, in many African American homes discipline is confined to one moment. It is also confusing for African American children to be told in an emotional moment that they are grounded for 30 days, but before they can bat an eye, they are outside playing. It is imperative that African American parents be more consistent with discipline and never state a punishment that cannot or will not be enforced.

Parents, in defense of their child's behavior, will say, "I don't understand why he acts that way with you because he respects me." Because they have not been taught the village concept, the parent has not taught the child to respect all neighbors, teachers, and other adults in the community. The child has a selective respect for discipline.

The questioning communication style of middle-class teachers is also a source of problems. "Isn't it time for you to begin doing you math problems? Isn't it time for you to begin to straighten up your desk?" In middle-class culture, adults like to communicate with children in the form of suggestions. It is their attempt to teach children to be self-disciplined. In many African American homes, parents do not make suggestions. They give directives. They say, "Boy, go take your bath, go to bed, and empty the garbage." The problem is that if children are reared in

African American Parents

households where parents make direct statements and go to schools where teachers make suggestions, teachers believe the children are being defiant when they don't respond. Children unused to receiving suggestions believe that so far no one has "told me what to do." From the teacher's perspective, if you ask someone to do something, you run the risk that they might answer in the negative.

I've often said that I can visit a house and in five minutes determine the kind of child coming out of that house. I believe basketball players need different things in their homes from engineers and doctors. If I visited your house, what would I see? Listed are some of the items that I look for in a house that values education:

- dictionary
- thesaurus
- calculator
- atlas
- globe
- books
- library card
- Scrabble
- Password
- checkers
- chess
- encyclopedia set
- musical instrument
- microscope
- chemistry set
- computer with Internet access

Many African American families have more CDs than books. I have observed households where every bedroom has a television. Some principals have told me tragic stories of parents coming into their office and informing them that they don't have a dollar for the field trip while smoking a cigarette in the principal's face! Middle-class teachers believe that Black people buy what they want and beg for what they need. How do we explain a car loan note being more important than rent? Shouldn't the house come before the car? How do we explain poor Whites in trailer homes being connected to the Internet while many affluent African Americans aren't?

We must do better. But how can we do better if we've never been taught how to parent? Where in America do you learn how to parent? For most of us, it's trial and error and memories of how our parents raised us. There are schools to teach you how to become a doctor, engineer, accountant, or lawyer, but where do you learn how to parent?

I would like you to take the following quiz from my book *Restoring The Village*. Grade yourself from an A to an F on each question. Grade yourself as rigorously as schools grade your children. I would then like you to have your children review your answers. Here is the quiz:

Grade

— Have you taught your children about God, His word, and the power of prayer?
— Do your children have goals?
— Do you provide quality time?
— Do you praise more than you criticize?
— How well do you listen to your children?
— Are you consistent?
— Do you give them high expectations?

African American Parents

— Do you teach your children African history?
— Have you provided your children with a nutritious diet?
— Do you monitor homework?
— Do you select, discuss, and monitor television shows?
— Do you know your children's friends and their values?
— Could your children develop a family tree?
— Do your children receive adequate sleep?
— Do you take your children on field trips?
— How frequently do you visit your child's school?
— Do you listen and discuss your children's music selections?
— How disciplined are your children?
— How well do your children complete chores?
— How frequently do you hug your children?
— Have you provided a safe environment for your children?[27]

Read the excellent book by Reginald Clark, *Family Life and School Achievement*. Clark was frustrated with the rumor that low-income, single African American parents could not produce high-achieving students. In his exhaustive study, he looked at African American middle-income and low-income families as well as single-parent and two-parent families. His research determined that it was not the number of parents or the amount of money in the home. What Clark identified were five traits that made the difference between high and low achievement: The quality of the interaction, belief of parents that they were the primary educators, high parental expectations, the transmission of hope, and consistency.[28]

Sonya Carson, the mother of Dr. Ben Carson, is the perfect illustration of Clark's research. She simply turned off the television and made Ben read and write a weekly book report. She was unable to read, so she drew upon the "village" and had her sister read the report.

African American children lead the country with 30 hours per week of television viewing. Many low-income parents have four televisions or more in their homes. We could close the achievement gap if African American families would turn off the television for two hours each weekday night in favor of reading. What will it take for African Americans to do something so simple? Jesse Jackson, Sr., has requested this for almost two decades. The government cannot legislate this. It requires a commitment from parents. Many White affluent kindergarten children arrive on the first day with over 1,000 hours in literacy compared with some African American children who have less than 25 hours involvement with books.

The problem could be that children need role models. It would be hypocritical for parents to implore their children to turn off television while parents continually watch. Children need parents who love reading enough to turn off the television. Parents must also be aware that 80 percent of what children learn during the school year is lost during the summer without academic reinforcement.

I am very concerned with the math disparity between the races. Upper-grade African American youth are doing very poorly in math. There are many factors contributing to this dilemma, but in this chapter for parents, I implore you to never tell your children you were not good in math or you did not like it. Children begin to think their failure is genetically driven and its not relevant. Parents must encourage their children to reach their full math potential.

As we move into the last chapter, Models of Success, we will recap some strategies and offer new national models that can be implemented.

Chapter Eight

Models of Success

One of the things I enjoy most about being an author is doing the research: I get to read many schools of thought about particular issues. In this chapter, the models come from Africentric institutions like the Council of Independent Black Institutions (CIBI), Africentric charter schools, the National Association of Black School Educators (NABSE), the Heritage Foundation, The Brookings Institute, The Manhattan Research Think Tank, and many individual scholars with differing opinions.

I have no loyalty to any institution. I am not restricted by teacher unions, lobbyists, or any group of people whose positions are shaped by their particular interest. I have only one concern, namely, that every African American child deserves to receive a quality education. I do not care whether they are educated in a one-room school shack in South Carolina by Marva Collins or if they are educated by a White private school in an affluent suburb.

How can public school educators be against vouchers while sending their own children to private schools? My mentor Barbara Sizemore pursues change by looking not only at the problem but also at the causes of the problem. Once you identify the cause, you brainstorm solutions and then implement them.

Unfortunately, in a typical one-hour workshop, we allocate fifty-five minutes to the problem, four minutes to the cause, one minute to the solution, and we'll come back next year to discuss implementation. Many people love to dwell on the problem, whether in my workshops or in the teachers' lounge. If teachers blame poor student performance on low income, then a workshop on teacher expectations, time on-task, more right-brained lesson plans, a multicultural or Africentric curriculum, non-tracking classes, and positive peer pressure will not address the cause. The solutions vis-a-vis to the low-income theory begin with White America paying African Americans what they pay themselves and for African Americans to have a greater propensity for entrepreneurship.

If teachers believe that the major cause for the racial achievement gap is fatherlessness, then academic solutions will not address this cause. The only solution that will address this cause is to reduce the 66 percent divorce rate in Black America. It is also high in White America, hovering near 50 percent. It has always amazed me how teachers are critical of their students' family problems when all is not well in their own homes.

If teachers believe that the major reason for the achievement gap between African American and White children is genetics, then no solutions will address this cause because there is no way to change the genetic make up of African American children.

In this chapter, we will look at Success Models from a micro-perspective first and then expand to the macro-perspective. My reason for starting micro is that the first solutions will be easier to implement. They will require less money and less change to the existing structure.

The first solution comes from the excellent research of Ron Edmonds and his *Effective Schools Model* and the Heritage Foundation's *No More Excuses.*[29] They compiled a list of schools, public, private, and charter, that successfully educate low-income children of color, with the majority scoring above the national average. The salient factor in all these schools is that the principal is the instructional leader. These principals have either designated someone else to perform administrative functions or principals tax themselves to do that outside of the school day. When the children are present, they are visiting classrooms, observing teachers, and making suggestions.

The future of African American children lies in the hands of principals, who must monitor teachers. From a larger perspective, the future lies in the hands of the superintendent. Unfortunately, ineffective superintendents will not hold weak principals accountable. Ron Edmonds identified the following five major factors of effective schools:

1. The principal is the instructional leader.
2. Teachers have high expectations.
3. Students spend more time on task.
4. There is a positive school climate.
5. Testing is used to guide further instruction and not solely for evaluation.[30]

The Center for Research on the Education of Students Placed At-Risk (CRESPAR) at Howard University under the leadership of Wade Boykin developed the Talent Development Model to augment Edmonds' research. They want to expand school evaluation beyond a culturally biased, multiple-choice achievement test. They also want to measure academic motivation, social-emotional competence, attendance, and community involvement and awareness.

Jacqueline Irvine, a very respected educator, takes the position that in-service training is not going to change someone's values and beliefs but it can change behavior.[31] It is naive to believe that a 60-minute workshop can change values and beliefs. If a Referral Agent believes that African American children are inferior, in-service training is not going to change that mind set. I agree with Irvine in that in-service training can change behavior, but only if principals follow up with observation. Theory is validated by practice.

Progressive principals request that I present the workshop on one day, and allocate the second day to observation and practice. They clearly communicate the objectives and outcomes. It is very frustrating to provide a workshop on right-brain lesson plans, cooperative learning, and our Africentric curriculum, SETCLAE, and then see teachers return to their classrooms and make no changes. Janice Hale takes the position that the most important factor in the education of children is teacher accountability.[32] Principals must transform custodians, referral agents, and instructors or remove them.

I agree with Hale that it is the responsibility of the principal to monitor teachers. I also concur with Murrell that what matters are school's practices, not their policies or principles. Education is the only industry where everyone knows that bad teaching is a serious problem, yet the longer it goes on, the more compensation the teacher receives. Children will tell me that they had a good third grade teacher and a poor fourth grade teacher. Parents will tell me the same. Staff will tell me which teachers are Coaches and which are Custodians. The challenge is how to implement the recommendations of the National Commission on Teaching when unions protect incompetent teachers even when evidential video tape is provided. Further, who are principals going to replace incompetents with in light of the present teacher shortage? Black colleges, churches, fraternities, sororities, and educational organizations must respond.

Principals should consider implementing a mentoring program to improve the skills of Custodians, Referral Agents, and Instructors. There is a wealth of resources that are available within a school if only principals would draw upon their Master Teachers and Coaches. Teachers could also benefit from a buddy system. In low-achieving schools, teachers are islands unto themselves, but in high-achieving schools, they observe one another, offer suggestions, team teach, share lesson plans and materials. While I think educational consultants like myself can play a major role in helping schools close the achievement gap, I also believe mentoring is effective. Who knows what the school needs more than Coaches?

We cannot ignore the research of Dr. Dee and the positive impact African American teachers have on Black students. How can we deny a 4 percentage point annual test-score increase with African American teachers? A White Coach is more effective than an African American Custodian, but with all things being equal, we must implement Dee's research. The disparity between 7 percent African American teachers and 17 percent African American students is unacceptable.

I commend those states that have streamlined teacher requirements to attract adults from the corporate sector into the classroom. Many districts have provided wages compatible to corporations and a signing bonus. I strongly encourage every administrator to implement the Pathways to Teaching Careers Program. It focuses on recruiting older staff, paraprofessionals, and private-sector personnel desirous of a career change. Pathways' success surpasses traditional methods of recruiting African American staff. If we live in a capitalistic country where money is valued and we have an acute shortage of African American teachers, specifically male, we should streamline the process and provide financial incentives.

How do we close the achievement gap? Several states and colleges initiatives to increase the number of African American teachers, particularly African American males. I commend Clemson, Wichita State, Jackson State, Northern Illinois, and Marygrove College in Detroit. There are 1,464 senior colleges in 50 states and they all need to have programs and financial incentives to increase the number of African American teachers. If the federal government is serious about "Leaving no child behind," the bureaucrats need to read Dee's work and provide four-year scholarships to all qualified African American students interested in teaching. We need African American educators to encourage their own biological children and their students to pursue education. We need White principals to stop complaining that they can't find any African American teachers and appoint an African American staff member to work with Black colleges, fraternities, sororities, and Black churches to identify candidates.

As mentioned earlier, the study "Good Teaching Matters" reports that effective teachers supersede, race, income, gender, and family demographics. Did the teacher pass the state competency exam? What was the teachers college GPA? Did the teacher major in the subject that he or she is teaching? Over his or her career, what has been the performance of his or her students? How can we ensure that low-income African American children will receive quality teaching? It is one thing to say that we will "leave no child behind," but what will federal, state, and local governments do to ensure that there is an equitable distribution of quality teachers throughout the country? High-quality teaching matters, but do we have the commitment to implement this axiom for the benefit of all children?

We must change the way college education departments prepare teachers. I often wonder if professors of education have ever taught in an inner city public school. How can you, as a professor at a college in the rural part of the state, educate aspiring teachers who live in that same region and do their student teaching in that region to be successful in the inner city? If we are going to be successful at closing the racial achievement gap, we must revamp most education departments. I've spoken to many school districts, but I seldom speak to education departments.

Models of Success

Are education departments preparing teachers to work with right-brained learners? Are they preparing teachers to properly channel Black male energy? Are they preparing teachers to use a street-based curriculum to teach reading and math? Are they preparing teachers to work with *Leave it to Beaver* children or *Bebe's Kids*? We have actually designed schools for *Leave it to Beaver* children not *Bebe's Kids*? Some teachers who are reading this book may not know about *"Bebe's Kids"* because they did not see the movie—but their students did.

I mentioned earlier that everyone knows where the problems and solutions lie. Many teachers have told me that even without having read "Good Teaching Matters" they know that if their students could receive three consecutive years of teaching from Coaches, it would make a major difference in their lives. It is very frustrating for a Coach to have to surrender his or her second-grade students to a third-grade Custodian or Referral Agent. Most children are not resilient enough to ward off the negative impact of one year under a Custodian or Referral Agent. Many principals have told me they place their stronger teachers in the upper grades because weaker teachers cannot manage the students. This is such a Band-Aid approach. I suggest that Master Teachers be placed in the earlier grades; that is where we lose students.

As stated earlier, two consecutive years of ineffective teachers can destroy a child for the rest of his or her life. African American students are victimized by the "volleyball effect"—bouncing back and forth between Coaches and Custodians. It can be worse when African American students have consecutive, if not all their years, with Custodians, Referral Agents, and Instructors. The concept of "serial teaching" can help. It requires principals to design classes in such a way that a particular group of students, preferably the lowest-achieving group, will have three consecutive years with Coaches and Master Teachers. Hopefully, as result of this experience, more and more teachers within the building will be challenged to realize that the problem is not with the students but with the quality of teaching and this will inspire them to become better in their profession.

A similar option to serial teaching is "looping." This allows a teacher to matriculate with one class for several years. This is ideal for African American students, where bonding is essential. Unfortunately, it would be catastrophic if the students were looped with Custodians, Referral Agents, or Instructors.

I also mentioned earlier the Nguzo Saba Assembly. The founder of Kwanzaa, Maulana Karenga, believes, the major problem in Black America is a lack of Africentric values. Priorities are skewed as well. Schools place more value on athletics than academic achievement. Schools hold athletic assemblies in which athletes are rewarded with large trophies, but in academic assemblies students are given buttons and pins. Earlier, we cited that a major problem among African American students is negative peer pressure and the feeling that being smart is acting White. We must adjust academic assembly programs to an Africentric perspective. The Nguzo Saba Assembly becomes the answer to this problem. The Assembly creates the opportunity for everyone to receive an award. If a student moves from a D to a C, he will receive one award. If he moves from a C to an A, he receives two awards. The Nguzo Saba Assembly develops self-esteem and a love of academic achievement.

In two of my earlier books, *Countering the Conspiracy to Destroy Black Boys* and *State of Emergency*, we provided

Models of Success

numerous solutions for schools to help close the achievement gap. The list includes the following:

- Mandatory in-service training for teachers on Black male learning styles.

- A Booker T. Washington/W.E.B. Dubois role model program.

- A Rites of Passage program.

- A fourth-grade intervention team (ministers, social workers, community activists entrepreneurs, and psychologists).

- A moratorium on placing African males in special education (unless there's a physical reason such as a lack of hearing, sight, or limb function).

- Increase Black male teacher assistants.

- Increase Black male teachers.

- A Dr. King class on nonviolence.

- A Malcolm X class for those assigned to in-house suspensions.

- A right-brained classroom.

- Black male and female classrooms (Over 500 schools have created single gender classrooms and report less suspensions and teen pregnancies, and a increase in test scores).

- A Black male and female school[33]

Currently, the burden of education is on the parent and child. While I am not in favor of social promotion and I have major problems with a parent criticizing a teacher for retaining their child who could not read beyond grade level, I also believe it is unfair for a child to be retained while the teaching environment remains backward and unchanging. If the child failed because of low expectations, inadequate time on task, left-brained lesson plans, an irrelevant Eurocentric curriculum, or negative peer pressure, why should we expect better results next term, using the same format? If we are going to retain the child for another year, some if not all of those variables need to change. It is insane to repeat the same mistakes and expect improvement. Therefore, my recommendation is that when a child is retained, the school is required to create a different paradigm in the subsequent year.

If we are going to successfully educate all children, we must do something about the elitist system called tracking. Tracking is beneficial to teachers but detrimental to the majority of children. If we are going to play God and divide children based on ability, then why, if we are interested in educating all children, do we allocate the best resources and best teachers to the higher-achieving students? Are we trying to widen or close the gap? It has always frustrated me that superintendents and principals invite me to their schools under the assumption that they want to close the achievement gap, yet they maintain tracking. One of the major reasons for the achievement gap is because schools track students based on ability and allocate greater resources to the higher-achieving group. My recommendation is that we "un-track" schools. Tracking benefits only the few.

One tremendous success model is the Knowledge is Power Program (Kipp) Academy. Their program started with two young White males who were innocent and naive enough to believe that all children can learn and that race, income, and marital status are not the major issues. The program started in Houston, expanded to New York, and is now being implemented nationwide. Their success is predicated on only two factors. First, educators must be Coaches. Second, and the most important element of the Kipp Academy, more time must be spent on task. They understand the secrets to success. As a result, the Kipp Academy has a longer school day, half a day on Saturday, and an expanded school year. It is amazing that America thinks it can compete with Germany and Japan, which offer 220 and 200 school days per year, respectively, when we only offer 180 annual school days.

Teachers who taught in regular schools where they were frustrated now teach at Kipp Academy, work longer hours, and feel satisfied. I strongly recommend that every principal and staff member visit a Kipp Academy. They will realize that the major factor affecting academic achievement is time on task.

The Council of Independent Black Institutions (CIBI) is another tremendous success story. They don't receive enough publicity but I understand it is because of their strong Africentric position. Before vouchers and charter schools became popular, these independent African-oriented schools were quietly educating African American children successfully. This association of more than forty schools is committed not only to transferring skills to African American children but also to immersing them in their history and culture. Before the national emphasis on infusing the curriculum to be more Africentric, CIBI had created a curriculum. CIBI students are not bored. They see themselves in the curriculum. In an earlier chapter, we mentioned that the curriculum should prepare students to solve everyday problems. CIBI's staff and curriculum has created a perfect marriage between theory and practice, between school and community. CIBI teaches their students to be self-reliant and value Black nationalism. Students are taught to see the relationship between family and nation. CIBI starts their children historically five million years ago rather than in 1619. They fully understand the distinction between African and Negro history. CIBI students are taught that the acquisition of skills is not designed for their personal aggrandizement but are to be returned to the community for its empowerment.

Black colleges are also great success models. There are over 1,464 colleges in America, of which only 106 are Black colleges. These Black colleges only have 16 percent of the African American college student population, but they produce almost 30 percent of African American college graduates. What explains their success? Why is it that some schools just admit you and other schools help you graduate? People who suffer from racism and the bell curve might think that the reason for the disparity between 16 and 30 percent is because it's easier to graduate from a Black college. If that's true, meditate on the following statistic. Almost 75 percent of African Americans who go on to earn a Master's or Doctorate degree were undergraduates at Black colleges! If Black colleges are inferior, how could their students go on to Princeton, Yale, and Harvard for graduate degrees? More importantly, Black colleges inspire students to secure graduate degrees. Many African American youth have been so frustrated and their spirits so broken at White colleges that they either do not graduate or feel so shattered after the experience that they choose not to pursue a graduate degree.

Models of Success

What can we learn from Black colleges that we can apply in the kindergarten through twelfth grade experience? I wonder if African American students at Morehouse, Spelman, Howard, North Carolina A & T, FAMU, and elsewhere tease each other when they are doing well and accuse each other of acting White. I wonder about the impact of having a faculty that is more than 50 percent African American in contrast to White colleges where the percentage is less than 5 percent. How does it feel to be the only African American student in the class, as opposed to being in a class that is primarily or all African American?

African American students need more African American faculty. We mentioned in the introductory material on Trends that African American students represent 17 percent of the student population at the K through 12 level, but African American teachers only represent 7 percent. That figure will decline to 5 percent in the near future. We can learn from Black colleges that when African American students are in the majority, it's a nurturing environment and peer pressure can be positive and can reinforce academic achievement.

One of my major regrets concerning Black colleges is their lack of commitment to infusing the curriculum and making it more Africentric. Nevertheless, they continue to tell me that they try to infuse Africentricity into all courses. In actuality, some schools have been more successful than others. In fact, White colleges such as Temple, the University of Wisconsin, Michigan, Ohio State, and the University of California have strong African American studies programs.

Another success model that we need to learn from is showcased in the research of the Students/Teachers Achievement Ratio (STAR). It provides the most definitive findings yet on the effects of reducing class size vis-a-vis student achievement. In 1985 the STAR project started a longitudinal study in Tennessee that followed kindergarten through third-grade students who were placed in small classes of between 13 and 17 students. The control group attended regular-size classes. The study monitored both groups' reading and math achievement each year. Students who had been assigned to the smaller classes scored significantly higher on reading and math tests. A follow-up study found that when the STAR students reached eighth grade, those who had been in smaller classes up to third grade continued to out-perform the control group. Minority students achieved the greatest gains. A later follow-up study of STAR students found that by high-school graduation, children originally in smaller classes showed superior educational outcomes than peers in larger classes. Throughout their school careers, STAR students continued to show higher levels of achievement, better grade point averages, and higher rates of on-time graduation. The students in smaller classes were also more likely to graduate in the top 25 percent of the class, less likely to drop out, and more likely to attend college.

The effect of class-size reduction was also studied in Milwaukee's Student Achieving and Guarantee in Education program (SAGE). They reported gains similar to those of STAR. SAGE reported that the largest academic gains for African American males were in smaller classes. Another similar study of 200 school districts found smaller class size raised math achievement by six months, with low-income students living in urban areas making the largest gains.

The National Black Caucus of State Legislators in 2001 recommended that school districts establish a policy that limits class size to 17 students.[34] If the federal government is serious about "leaving no child behind," one of the first things that it needs to do is make sure that all children receive the same level of funding. Funding is needed in low-income school districts to

Models of Success

reduce class size. Ward Connerly and others need to acknowledge that affirmative action does exist in America, and it exists in the context of how we fund education. It is an embarrassment that children in the same state have such dramatic disparities in funding. In one district each child will receive $33,000; in another each will receive $3,300. This disparity is manifested at the most acute level in class size. Every effort must be made by every school district to reduce the number of children in classrooms. Unfortunately, there are many schools with 34 children in a class, not withstanding STAR's and SAGE's research that shows the ideal number to be 17.

While I totally agree with Jonathan Kozol's book *Savage Inequalities*, how do we explain hundreds of poorly funded schools outperforming their wealthy counterparts? For example, in Illinois the Northbrook school district allocates $12,000 per child, and 91 percent of their students perform above the national average. Western Springs in the same state receives less that $6,000 per child, yet 93 percent of their students perform above the national average. What was Western Springs' secret? They utilized parents as tutors. Stono Park Elementary School in Charleston secured similar results by hiring a parent liaison to strengthen relationships and communication between school staff and parents.

Military schools turn out excellent students. Thirty-eight percent of military school students score above the national average in contrast to 24 percent in public schools nationwide. If our major objective is to close the racial achievement gap, there are no schools in the country that have demonstrated a greater success than military schools. The gap is smaller in military schools than in any other schools in the country. Presently, there are 120,000 students and 224 schools, with 40 percent of their students of color. What explains the success of military schools?

There are numerous factors. One is that the Department of Defense allocates $9,503 per student in comparison to the average public school per pupil expenditure of $7,682. The most significant factor in the success of military schools is not funding, however, but parent involvement. The Department of Defense encourages parents to be involved in the school and because of the campus-like atmosphere, a village effect is in existence and discipline is valued.

I also recommend James Comer's School Development Program. He believes there is too much division between staff, administrators, and parents. The program includes a parent, management, and staff support team. Comer believes that when people communicate more and share the same vision, everyone wins. The program is now in almost 1,000 schools.

The last success model that I want to mention comes from the Brookings Institute. They along with the Manhattan Institute and numerous think tanks have been advocating that vouchers can benefit African American children. Presently, there are more than 70,000 children receiving public or private vouchers. Depending upon the studies you read, it can become very complicated and convoluted with regard to the success of vouchers. The Supreme Court ruled in June, 2002, that it is constitutional for religious schools to accept public vouchers. Of course, when the battle lines were drawn, teacher unions were against vouchers. Again I ask, how can public school teachers be against vouchers when many send their own biological children to private schools? If you had the resources to send your child to a free but poor performing public school or an excellent private school, which would you choose? Interestingly, in this capitalistic and individualistic country that values competition– why is it that public schools are against competition and choice?

Models of Success

The Brookings Institute discovered that there are benefits to attending private schools. In a six-year study, they documented that there's a 17 times greater chance that African American children will attend a four-year college if they attended a private school. In addition, there is a 265-point differential among African American students on the SAT if they attended private schools.[35]

Public school advocates counter with the fact that 90 percent of private schools are very exclusive. In addition, Catholic schools deny 66 percent of their applicants. In Milwaukee, only 38 percent of private schools provide transportation. Over the past decade, there has been an increase of only 1,359 African Americans enrolled in private schools, while their public school attendance has increased by 4,419. Voucher legislation has failed in California and Michigan. Only 12 percent of White Americans favor vouchers, and ironically, only 5 percent of African Americans.

Some voucher critics feel it is a moot point because the Black community does not have the infrastructure and resources to privately educate more than 10 million children. What number can CIBI accept? How many students could churches like Allen AME in Queens, New York, pastored by my friend Floyd Flake accommodate? Historically, Catholic schools were successful in the African American community because the church filled the budget gap and a good percentage of staff were nuns. This is no longer the case. Tuitions have risen, and many schools have closed. The 2002 Supreme Court decision on vouchers will benefit religious schools.

The major challenge with CIBI has always been financial. They have a committed staff, they understand African American children's learning styles, and their curriculum is relevant. But the reality is that once you become private, you must charge tuition. Unfortunately, the very families CIBI wanted to empower cannot pay the tuition. CIBI has been suffering from inadequate revenue to pay their staff salaries commensurate to those of public schools.

One compromise bridging the gap between public and private schools has been the explosion of charter schools. Just a decade ago, there were only two charter schools in America. Presently, we are hovering near 3,000, which educate more than a half million students. A 1997 national survey of nearly 5,000 charter pupils revealed impressive satisfaction. They cited good teachers (59 percent) who teach until I learn (51 percent), they don't let me fall behind (39 percent), they offer technology (36 percent), class size is low (34 percent), and curriculum is relevant (33 percent). The average size elementary charter school has 137 students in contrast to 475 students in regular schools. School organizational research confirms that the ideal high school should not exceed 500 students. When this occurs, achievement and attendance improve while suspension and dropout rates decline.[36]

The federal government has reinterpreted its strict position on single-gender schools and Title IX legislation. They are encouraging more schools to implement single-gender classrooms. I predict a tremendous increase in single-gender charter schools over the next decade. The Thurgood Marshall Elementary School in Seattle implemented a male classroom and saw discipline referrals drop from 30 to 2 per day. They also observed a 63 percent increase of males satisfying state academic standards.[37]

To remain fiscally solvent, some CIBI schools have become charter schools. This decision partners them with the very institution with which they had political differences. CIBI continues to wrestle internally with this political issue.

We need scholars and master and doctoral students to research the Minority Student Achievement Network (MSAN); Whitney Young H. S. in Chicago; Prince George's County, Maryland;

Models of Success

Mt. Vernon, New York; and Philadelphia. Each program warrants a book. How do we explain middle- and upper-class African American children whose achievement gap is wider than that of their lower-class counterparts? Community leaders in these neighborhoods are puzzled at the sparse percentage attending college.

While MSAN grapples with middle-class students' unacceptable performance, the reality is that their children attend schools where they are the minority and there is a paucity of African American teachers. How do we explain neighborhoods like Prince George's County that are not only affluent but also politically controlled by African Americans? The operative word is "politically". African Americans may be the mayor, superintendent of education, chief of police, and fire chief, but economically, much is left to be desired in that county.

In spite of Dee's research, African American achievement has not been stellar. Race cannot explain Blacks' abysmal performance. While class dynamics are a factor, how can we explain middle-income African American teachers mis-educating middle-income African American students? Throughout this book, I have written about the demons of low expectations, poor time on task, incongruence between pedagogy and learning styles, irrelevant curricula, negative peer pressure, tracking, and poor parent involvement.

In the inner city of Chicago, Whitney Young is considered one of the best schools, not just in the city, but the state. It is a magnet school that draws the best students in the city. While I'm not in favor of magnet schools because of their elitist nature, I wish to include them because they receive less money than their state counterparts, but their test scores are in the state elite. How do "funding" advocates reconcile that fact? Their student-teacher ratio is also larger than their state peers. What makes the difference? Besides drawing the best students, their staff is excellent, and negative peer pressure is reduced due to a high proportion of academically high-achieving African American students. It is an integrated school, and African American students are academically competitive. I believe every major city has a Whitney Young that needs to be studied and replicated system wide.

How do we explain the success in Mt. Vernon, New York? In 1998 only 33 percent of their fourth graders met state standards, but in 2001 it soared to 77 percent! Some schools started with only 12 percent at grade level, yet they rose to 90 percent! Three of their schools were recognized as the best in the entire state. The answer lies with leadership. The superintendent, Ronald Ross, asserts, "There's nothing wrong with public education except the leadership that underestimates our young people." He hired staff to relieve principals of mundane administrative assignments such as monitoring lunchrooms and bus schedules. Principals use their time to be the instructional leaders of the school.[38]

Lastly, while this book was in progress, Philadelphia schools were taken over by the state and parceled out primarily to White corporations. So now, the future of the Black race lies in the hands of White female teachers and White corporations like Edison. What is the state of Black leadership that it would allow this to happen in a school district where more than 80 percent of the students are Black and Hispanic? What do our children think of us?

Ron Edmonds challenged us decades ago with these profound words, "We can whenever, and wherever, we choose, successfully teach all children whose schooling is of interest to us. We already know more than we need to do that. Whether or not we do it must finally depend on how we feel about the fact that we haven't so far."

Glossary

African triangle: Africa, Central-South America, North America.

Africentric: a person or program that interprets ideas from an African perspective.

Classics: the best in literature and music, transcending a specific time.

Classism: a negative bias toward someone due to their income level.

Culture: a people's values, ethos, and worldview that dictate their lifestyle, which includes their form of worship, clothing, diet, language, child rearing, recreation, holidays, etc.

Educational assimilation: Black schools close, their principals become teachers, their students are bused, the curriculum remains Eurocentric, and the pedagogy continues to be left-brained.

Educational integration: busing involves all students, the curriculum and pedagogy become multicultural, and staffing reflects the racial make-up of the school.

Eurocentric: a person or program that interprets ideas from a European perspective.

High-stakes testing: discriminates against remedial and special education students whose curriculum does not parallel the test. In addition, it hinders students in poorly funded schools with unqualified and inexperienced teachers.

Household: the total number of people living in the dwelling. Thirty-three percent of African American households live below the poverty line, but 50 percent of African American children. In contrast, 25 percent of African American households earn in excess of $50,000 while only 8 percent of African American children live in households earning the above figure. Many affluent African American households are childless or have very few.

Maafa: African holocaust in which an estimated 30-60 million Africans died in the African triangle between 1400-1920.

Maat: seven cardinal virtues, they include truth, justice, order, harmony, balance, righteousness, and reciprocity.

Multicultural: a person or program that interprets ideas by reconciling the views of all races and ethnic groups.

Nguzo Saba: seven principles of Blackness, they include unity, self-determination, collective work and responsibility, cooperative economics, purpose, creativity, and faith.

Prejudice: an unsubstantiated negative bias toward someone primarily due to race.

Racism: the act or policy of discriminating against those of another race due to prejudice.

Sexism: a negative bias toward someone due to their gender.

Tracking: dividing students based on test scores into homogeneous groups.

References

1. *U.S. Statistical Abstract 2001.* Frederick Patterson Research Institute, Just the Facts, 2001.

2. Payne, Ruby. *A Framework for Understanding Poverty.* Highland Texas: Aha, 2001, pp. 42-45.

3. Howard, Gary. *We Can't Teach What We Don't Know.* New York: Teachers College Press, 1999, p. 109.

4. Delpit, Lisa. *Other People's Children.* New York: New Press, 1995, pp. 115-116, 142.

5. Dee, Thomas. "Teachers, Race and Student Achievement," *National Bureau of Economic Research.* August, 2001, No.W8432.

6. op. cit., Delpit, p. 167.

7. Ladson-Billings, Gloria. *Dreamkeepers.* San Francisco: Jossey-Bass, 1994, pp. 21-23.

8. Haycock, Kati. "Good Teaching Matters," *Thinking K-16 by Education Trust.* Summer 1998, pp. 1-10.

9. Hess, Frederick. *Revolution at the Margins.* Washington: Brookings Institute, 2002, pp. 67-68, 80, 93-94.

10. Kunjufu, Jawanza. *Developing Positive Self Images and Discipline in Black Children.* Chicago: African American Images, 1997, pp. 57-60.

11. Reglin, Gary. *Motivating Low-Achieving Students.* Springfield, Illinois: Charles Thomas, 1993, pp. 28-29.

12. Hunter, Madeline. *Mastery Teaching*. El Segundo, California: Tip Publications, 1982, p. 5.

13. Haberman, Martin. "The Pedagogy of Poverty vs. Good Teaching," *Phi Delta Kappan*. December 1991, pp. 290-294.

14. Canfield, Jack. *Chicken Soup for the Teacher's Soul*. Deerfield Beach, Florida: Health Communications, 2002, pp. 170-173.

15. op. cit., Payne, pp. 46-48.

16. op. cit., Delpit, p. 55.

17. Hale, Janice. *Learning While Black*. Baltimore: Johns Hopkins University Press, 2001, p. 46.

18. op. cit., Payne, p. 18.

19. Shade, Barbara. *Culture, Style and the Educative Process*. Springfield, Illinois: Charles Thomas, 1997, pp. 135-139.

20. op. cit., Kunjufu. *Developing Positive Self Images*, p. 40.

21. op. cit., Delpit, pp. 34-35.

22. op. cit., Payne, p. 103.

23. Kunjufu, Jawanza. *To Be Popular or Smart*. Chicago: African American Images, 1988, pp. 13-14, 44-49.

24. Kunjufu, Jawanza. *Satan, I'm Taking Back My Health*. Chicago: African American Images, 2000, p. 20.

25. Skiba, Russell. *The Color of Discipline*. Indiana Education Policy Center, Report #SR51, June 2000.

26. op. cit., Payne, pp. 37, 100.

27. Kunjufu, Jawanza. *Restoring the Village: Solutions for the Black Family.* Chicago: African American Images, 1996, p. 109.

28. Clark, Reginald. *Family Life and School Achievement.* Chicago: University of Chicago Press, 1983, p. 200.

29. Carter, Samuel. *No Excuses.* Washington: Heritage Foundation, 2001, pp. 7-11.

30. Edmonds, Ron. "Effective Schools for the Urban Poor," *Education Leadership.* 37:15-23. pp. 7-11.

31. Irvine, Jacqueline. *Black Students and School Failure.* New York: Praeger, 1990, p. 116.

32. op. cit., Hale, p. 182.

33. Kunjufu, Jawanza. *State of Emergency.* Chicago: African American Images, 2001, pp. 175-176.

34. National Black Caucus of State Legislators. "Closing the Achievement Gap," *Education Report* 2001, pp. 18-22.

35. Howell, William. *The Education Gap.* Washington: Brookings Institute, 2002, pp. 168-184. Green, Jay. "The Effect of School Choice." The Manhattan Institute, August 2000, No. 12.

36. Peterson, Paul, editor. *Charters, Vouchers, and Public Education.* Washington: Brookings Institute, 2001, pp. 23-24, 32.

37. *Education Week.* May 15, 2002, p. 24.

38. Price, Hugh. *Achievement Matters.* New York: Dafina, 2002, pp. 190-193.

Index. . .

Lucas, Tamara; 25
Manhattan Research Think Tank; 135,150
Mathematics; 61,106
Mbiti, John, 112
McCarthy, Bernice; 97-98
McNutt, Kevin; 102
Merit pay; 79
Military schools; 149-150
Milwaukee Public Schools; 60,151
Minority Student Achievement Network (MSAN); 36,152-153
Moses, Robert; 61
Mrosla, Helen; 80
Mt. Vernon New York; 154
Muhammad, Shahid; 61
Multiculturalism; 20,24
Murray, Charles; 48,70,94-95
Murrell, Jr. Peter; 16,70,110,138
NAACP Act-SO program, 115
National Association of Black School Educators (NABSE); 135
National Black Caucus of State Legislators; 148
National Center for Restructuring Education; 103
National Commission on Teaching; 78,138
National Teachers' Exam (NTE); 59
Nguzo Saba Assembly program; 114-115,142
Oakland Schools; 19
Oakes, Jeannie; 9
Ogbu, John; 109-110
Orr, Eleanor; 61,106
Paley, Vivian; 21,27,31
Pathways; 139
Payne, Ruby; 7,96,105,112,129
Peer pressure; 107,112-115

30% Pre-publication discount
Coming Soon!

An African Centered Response to Ruby Payne's
Poverty Theory
$11.15 * FREE Shipping

School Sets

Educators' Library * 22 BOOKS * $199.95

Black History Curriculum (SETCLAE)
67 BOOKS, teachers' manual and other products * $595.00 (specify grade)

Hispanic History and Culture * 40 BOOKS * $320.00

Biographies * 49 BOOKS cloth $1,499.95

Multicultural Videos * (20) * $595.00

Hip Hop Street Curriculum (Motivation - Self-Esteem)
80 BOOKS and teachers' manual $499.95 (specify grade)

Parent Set * 22 BOOKS * $199.95

Male - In-house suspension set * 50 BOOKS * $399.95 (specify grade)

Female - In-house suspension set * 50 BOOKS * $399.95 (specify grade)

Poster Set * (230) * $399.99

(Free Shipping)

AFRICAN AMERICAN IMAGES, INC.
Call: (773) 445-0322
Fax: (773) 445-9844
customer@africanamericanimages.com
www.africanamericanimages.com
1900 W. 95th St., Chicago, Illinois 60643